Fully In Focus

A Scriptural Collection Illustrating the Attributes of God

By
Carol Graves

www.FullyInFocus.com

PRESS

www.xulonpress.com

You will keep in perfect peace
all who trust in You —
all whose thoughts are
fixed (focused) on You.
        Isaiah 26:3 (NLT)

I pray that you are
blessed as you focus
on the fullness of God.
        Carol Graves

INTRODUCTION

S everal years ago, I bought an inexpensive telescope for
my son. He was just about the age when young boys
want to explore the skies and this seemed to be the perfect
tool for him to see deep into the universe. We chose a night
when the moon was full and bright and waited until darkness
had settled in. As we pointed the new telescope toward the
huge white ball in the sky and looked through the eyepiece,
we saw nothing but darkness.

We tried adjusting the position of the telescope, moving
it up and down and from side to side, trying to line it up with
what seemed to be an easy target. Finding it, however, was
not as easy as we thought. Even the slightest movement of
the telescope translated into a broad sweep of the sky, taking
our field of vision far from what we wanted to see.

After several tries, there it was – a blur of light in the
field of vision. We knew that we were now looking in the
right place, however the image was not in focus. Trying to
hold the position steady was no easy task, and we adjusted
the knobs, slowly bringing the moon into focus. What had
seemed to be just a big white ball in the sky, now clearly had
all kinds of attributes we had never seen before. There were
craters and maria of all sizes and shapes. There were hills
and shadows. Even the shape of the moon became much
clearer as we looked at how the edges tapered off. We were

amazed at what we saw, realizing that there was so much more to see than we had ever imagined. Yet, throughout our session, we had to carefully, steadily hold the telescope and adjust the focus to maintain a clear view of our treasure in the sky. Keeping fully in focus was not an easy task.

In recent years I have learned a transforming concept that has given me renewed confidence as I pray and peace as I wait upon God. The concept is simple. In order to find peace of mind and spirit, I must be able to keep fully focused on God. Yet, just as it was difficult for my son to keep the telescope focused on the moon, I find that it is even more difficult to keep my focus on the one who is able to meet my needs.

When I am anxious about my children, when I have concerns about finances or relationships, I tend to focus on myself, the needs of those I love, my circumstances, or any of those other things that scream for my attention throughout each day. Yet the only way I can find peace is to focus on God and who he is. That is when I find peace. As I focus on who he is, I see that he is faithful, he is able, he is forgiving, he is truth, he is strong, he is my comforter, he is my peace – and I could go on and on. By focusing on who he is, everything else falls into perspective.

Yet, often, though I know that God is near, it is like looking at the moon without the telescope. Although I see him, my focus is not clear enough to see all that he is.

So, how can I improve my focus on him? I have found that the best way is to study his attributes and to praise him for all that he is. I have learned this through a Moms In Touch International prayer group that I have attended for several years, but the concept applies to everyone. In order to become fully focused, first identify one of the attributes of God and read its definition. Then read and meditate on scriptures that illustrate the attribute. This sets the stage for praise. As you take time to praise God you experience how he expresses that attribute in your personal life and this brings your heart and mind fully in focus on him. As the focus shifts from self to God there is a realization that there is nothing you will face, no concern you will have that God is not fully able to handle.

This focus is sharpened through reading and studying God's Word, through singing praises to him, through fellowship with other Christ followers, even through observing the wonders of his creation – like looking at the moon through a telescope. As I do these things, I come to realize that he is everything and I am nothing. Yet, though I am nothing, as I keep my focus on him – all things are possible. That is where I find peace.

I vividly remember one morning as I was driving to work, I was extremely anxious for my daughter. That day she would be taking one final math test that she was required to pass in order to receive credit for a course she had taken by correspondence. Math had been extremely difficult for her. We had worked through all the lessons, worked every problem, practiced for the test, and still I was not sure how things would turn out. As I prayed for her, I remember pleading with God to help her remember all the things needed in order to pass. As I prayed, God spoke to my heart saying, "Do not focus on what your child can do, focus on who I am and what I can do." With that came immediate peace, for I knew that God is faithful, God is able, God is the source of wisdom, God is all knowing, and most of all God is in control. As I focused on all those attributes, I knew that my daughter would be fine. I was able to rest and rejoice in who God is. When the test results came back a few days later, she had made an A on the test! Yet, my peace came before knowing the test results. My peace came by focusing on God.

If you find yourself filled with doubt, anxious, and fearful about things that surround you, if all you see is darkness or just a blur of light, use the tools that will help sharpen your focus – prayer, praise, scripture, and fellowship with those who love God. Fully focus on God and all that he is. It will fill your heart with worship and your spirit with peace.

Focusing on Him,

Carol Graves

www.FullyInFocus.com

ACKNOWLEDGMENTS

I thank God for his living word that is so rich and full of
passages that illustrate his attributes, allowing us to see
who he is and teaching us to fully focus on him.

I thank my husband, my children and grandchildren for
their loving support, for believing in this project and for
encouraging me through the years as
I have prayed these verses for them.

I am so grateful for the Moms In Touch International orga-
nization and for the praying moms that I meet with each
week. The faithfulness of Janet Page and Suzie Buck who
serve God through this ministry has been life transforming
and has inspired me to focus on God and pray with confidence, trusting in his faithfulness.

How To Use This Book

This book is designed to assist you as you fully focus on God. In it you will find a collection of the attributes of God found throughout the Bible. Although they are infinite, I have chosen 52 – one for each week of the year. They are presented with a definition, brief personal observations, scriptures that illustrate that attribute, a scripture verse with blanks, and a final scripture.

Throughout each week I encourage you to read the definition, read and meditate on the scriptures, and take a few moments to praise God that he is the fulfillment of that attribute. Then, fully focused on God, read the verse with blanks, making it a prayer as you insert your name or the name of the person you are praying for. I believe you will find, as I have, that you will pray with more confidence and with a stronger faith as you keep your focus on God.

When you have finished praying, read the last verse as a blessing or encouragement to maintain your focus throughout the day. Then, throughout each day, observe how God applies that attribute to you personally. You will be amazed and blessed as you become keenly aware of how God is constantly at work in your life.

I pray that this book will bless you and that as you use it, you will experience the transforming peace that comes when God is fully in focus.

CONTENTS

God is Able

Able: having sufficient power, intelligence, competence, skill to accomplish action

How often do you find yourself facing a situation beyond your resources and beyond your control? It is during these times that our faith is tested to totally trust that God will work things out for good as he promises in his word. When the situation seems impossible, do you ask yourself, "Is God able?" The scriptures that follow should answer that question. In each situation, God was faithful and fully able to provide the perfect action revealing his power, intelligence, competence and skill. Enjoy reading these scriptures and be amazed that our God is able!

Genesis 1:1 In the beginning God created the heavens and the earth.

Genesis 22:9-14 When they reached the place God had told him about, Abraham built an altar there and arranged the wood on it. He bound his son Isaac and laid him on the altar, on top of the wood. Then he reached out his hand and took the knife to slay his son, but the angel of the LORD called out to him from heaven, "Abraham! Abraham!" "Here I am," he replied. "Do not lay a hand on the boy," he said.

"Do not do anything to him. Now I know that you fear God, because you have not withheld from me your son, your only son." Abraham looked up and there in a thicket he saw a ram caught by its horns. He went over and took the ram and sacrificed it as a burnt offering instead of his son. So Abraham called that place The LORD Will Provide. And to this day it is said, "On the mountain of the LORD it will be provided."

Genesis 37:23-24a So when Joseph came to his brothers, they stripped him of his robe — the richly ornamented robe he was wearing — and they took him and threw him into the cistern. **Genesis 41:41-43** So Pharoah said to Joseph, "I hereby put you in charge of the whole land of Egypt." Then Pharoah took his signet ring from his finger and put it on Joseph's finger. He dressed him in robes of fine linen and put a gold chain around his neck. He had him ride in a chariot as his second-in-command and men shouted before him, "Make way!" Thus he put him in charge of the whole land of Egypt.

Exodus 13:17-18 When Pharaoh let the people go, God did not lead them on the road through the Philistine country, though that was shorter. For God said, "If they face war, they might change their minds and return to Egypt." So God led the people around by the desert road toward the Red Sea. The Israelites went up out of Egypt armed for battle. **Exodus 14:21-22** Then Moses stretched out his hand over the sea, and all that night the LORD drove the sea back with a strong east wind and turned it into dry land. The waters were divided, and the Israelites went through the sea on dry ground, with a wall of water on their right and on their left.

Joshua 6:1, 15-16 Now Jericho was tightly shut up because of the Israelites. No one went out and no one came in. On the seventh day, they got up at daybreak and marched around the city seven times in the same manner, except that on that day they circled the city seven times. The seventh time around, when the priests sounded the trumpet blast, Joshua commanded the people, "Shout! For the LORD has given you the city!"

1 Samuel 17:45,48-50 David said to the Philistine, "You come against me with sword and spear and javelin, but I come against you in the name of the LORD Almighty, the God of the armies of Israel, whom you have defied. As the Philistine moved closer to attack him, David ran quickly toward the battle line to meet him. Reaching into his bag and taking out a stone, he slung it and struck the Philistine on the forehead. The stone sank into his forehead, and he fell facedown on the ground. So David triumphed over the Philistine with a sling and a stone; without a sword in his hand he struck down the Philistine and killed him.

Judges 6:15-16 "But Lord," Gideon asked, "how can I save Israel? My clan is the weakest in Manasseh, and I am the least in my family." The LORD answered, "I will be with you, and you will strike down all the Midianites together." **Judges 7:19-21** Gideon and the hundred men with him reached the edge of the camp at the beginning of the middle watch, just after they had changed the guard. They blew their trumpets and broke the jars that were in their hands. The three companies blew the trumpets and smashed the jars. Grasping the torches in their left hands and holding in their right hands the trumpets they were to blow, they shouted, "A sword for the LORD and for Gideon!" While each man held his position around the camp, all the Midianites ran, crying out as they fled.

Daniel 3:17 If we are thrown into the blazing furnace, the God we serve is able to save us from it, and he will rescue us from your hand, O king. **Daniel 3:26-27** Nebuchadnezzar then approached the opening of the blazing furnace and shouted, "Shadrach, Meshach and Abednego, servants of the Most High God, come out! Come here!" So Shadrach, Meshach and Abednego came out of the fire, and the satraps, prefects, governors and royal advisers crowded around them. They saw that the fire had not harmed their bodies, nor was a hair of their heads singed; their robes were not scorched, and there was no smell of fire on them.

Genesis 3:23-24 So the LORD God banished him (Adam) from the Garden of Eden to work the ground from which he had been taken. After he drove the man out, he placed on the east side of the Garden of Eden cherubim and a flaming sword flashing back and forth to guard the way to the tree of life. **Luke 23:46** Jesus called out with a loud voice, "Father, into your hands I commit my spirit." When he had said this, he breathed his last. **Romans 5:19** For just as through the disobedience of the one man the many were made sinners, so also through the obedience of the one man the many will be made righteous.

Hebrews 7:25 Therefore he (Jesus) is able to save completely those who come to God through him, because he always lives to intercede for them.

To him who is able to keep you, _____, from falling and to present you, _____, before his glorious presence without fault and with great joy — to the only God our

Savior be glory, majesty, power and authority, through Jesus Christ our Lord, before all ages, now and forevermore! Amen. Jude 1:24-25

Now to him who is able to do immeasurably more than all we ask or imagine, according to his power that is at work within us, to him be glory in the church and in Christ Jesus throughout all generations, for ever and ever! Amen. Ephesians 3: 20-21

God Abounds

Abound: to be present in large numbers or in great quantity; to be copiously (abundantly) supplied

Imagine a fish in an aquarium, then a fish in the ocean. One has a limited supply of water to swim in and the other has a supply that abounds. The fish in the ocean need never be concerned that the supply of water will be insufficient. The magnitude of that concept helps us understand the abounding love, grace and provision of God. My circumstance does not alter who God is. Though my needs may be great, he abounds in all the attributes that meet my needs. Consider the abounding nature of God and fill your heart with abounding praise.

Deuteronomy 6:3 Hear, O Israel, and be careful to obey so that it may go well with you and that you may increase greatly in a land flowing with milk and honey, just as the LORD, the God of your fathers, promised you.

Romans 5:20 The Law came in so that the transgression would increase; but where sin increased, grace abounded all the more. (New American Standard Bible)

Romans 10:12 For there is no distinction between Jew and Greek; for the same Lord is Lord of all, abounding in riches for all who call on Him. (New American Standard Bible)

Psalm 86:5 You are forgiving and good, O Lord, abounding in love to all who call to you.

Psalm 86:15 But you, O Lord, are a compassionate and gracious God, slow to anger, abounding in love and faithfulness.

Philippians 4:19-20 You can be sure that God will take care of everything you need, his generosity exceeding even yours in the glory that pours from Jesus. Our God and Father abounds in glory that just pours out into eternity. (The Message)

And God is able to make all grace abound to you, _ _____, so that in all things at all times, having all that you need, you, _____, will abound in every good work. 2 Corinthians 9:8

For this reason I kneel before the Father, from whom his whole family in heaven and on earth derives its name. I pray that out of his glorious riches he may strengthen you with power through his Spirit in your inner being, so that Christ may dwell in your hearts through faith. And I pray that you, being rooted and established in love, may have power, together with all the saints, to grasp how wide and long and high and deep is the love of Christ, and to know this love that surpasses knowledge — that you may be filled to the measure of all the fullness of God. Now to him who is able to do immeasurably more than all we ask or imagine, according to his power that is at work within us, to him be glory in the church and in Christ Jesus throughout all generations, for ever and ever! Amen. Ephesians 3: 14-21

God Binds our Wounds

Bind: to hold together

There are times that we must suffer wounds in order for healing to occur. When my husband broke his leg, it was shattered into many pieces. In order for the bones to heal, they first had to be put back together which required several surgeries. Though the doctors had to make wounds on his legs, each time they carefully bound the wounds so that they would heal completely. With each surgery, we became more focused on God's healing power and our hope grew that the leg would soon be healed.

We all experience times of trouble when we are wounded and brokenhearted. The scriptures tell us that God uses these times to teach us more about who he is and to help us focus on him. He alone is able to bind up those wounds and heal us completely. Look to him during difficult times and discover that he is the true source of hope. He is able and he is faithful to bind our wounds.

> **Job 5:17-19** Blessed is the man whom God corrects; so do not despise the discipline of the Almighty. For he wounds, but he also binds up; he injures, but his hands also heal. From six calamities he will rescue you; in seven no harm will befall you.

Isaiah 30:26 The moon will shine like the sun, and the sunlight will be seven times brighter, like the light of seven full days, when the LORD binds up the bruises of his people and heals the wounds he inflicted. **Psalm 147:3** He heals the brokenhearted and binds up their wounds. **Psalm 34:17-19** The righteous cry out, and the LORD hears them; he delivers them from all their troubles. The LORD is close to the brokenhearted and saves those who are crushed in spirit. A righteous man may have many troubles, but the LORD delivers him from them all.

Then your light, _____, will break forth like the dawn, and your healing, _____, will quickly appear; then your righteousness will go before you, _____, and the glory of the LORD will be your rear guard. Then you, _____, will call, and the LORD will answer; you will cry for help, and he will say: "Here am I." Isaiah 58:8-9a

The Spirit of the Sovereign LORD is on me, because the LORD has anointed me to preach good news to the poor. He has sent me to bind up the brokenhearted, to proclaim freedom for the captives and release from darkness for the prisoners, to proclaim the year of the Lord's favor and the day of vengeance of our God, to comfort all who mourn, and provide for those who grieve in Zion — to bestow on them a crown of beauty instead of ashes, the oil of gladness instead of mourning, and a garment of praise instead of a spirit of despair. They will be called oaks of righteousness, a planting of the LORD for the display of his splendor. Isaiah 61:1-3

God is Boundless

Boundless: having no bounds; unlimited; vast

In a world where there are boundaries of all kinds, it is very difficult to grasp the concept of a boundless God. He has no limits. There is no limit to his love, no limit to his forgiveness and no limit to his power. Be encouraged that when we pray, we pray to our God who has no limits.

Job 11:7-9 Can you fathom the mysteries of God? Can you probe the limits of the Almighty? They are higher than the heavens — what can you do? They are deeper than the depths of the grave — what can you know? Their measure is longer than the earth and wider than the sea.

Psalm 119:89-96 What you say goes, GOD, and stays, as permanent as the heavens. Your truth never goes out of fashion; it's as up-to-date as the earth when the sun comes up. Your Word and truth are dependable as ever; that's what you ordered — you set the earth going. If your revelation hadn't delighted me so, I would have given up when the hard times came. But I'll never forget the advice you gave me; you saved my life with those wise words. Save me! I'm all yours. I look high and low for your words of wisdom. The wicked lie in ambush to destroy me, but I'm only concerned with your plans for me. I see the limits to everything human, but the horizons can't contain your commands! (The Message)

Romans 11:33-36 Oh, the depth of the riches of the wisdom and knowledge of God! How unsearchable his judgments, and his paths beyond tracing out! Who has known the mind of the Lord? Or who has been his counselor? Who has ever given to God, that God should repay him? For from him and through him and to him are all things. To him be the glory forever! Amen.

Isaiah 9:6-7 For to us a child is born, to us a son is given, and the government will be on his shoulders. And he will be called Wonderful Counselor, Mighty God, Everlasting Father, Prince of Peace. Of the increase of his government and peace there will be no end. He will reign on David's throne and over his kingdom, establishing and upholding it with justice and righteousness from that time on and forever. The zeal of the LORD Almighty will accomplish this.

I ask — ask the God of our Master, Jesus Christ, the God of glory — to make you, _____, intelligent and discerning in knowing him personally, your eyes focused and clear, so that you, _____, can see exactly what it is he is calling you to do, grasp the immensity of this glorious way of life he has for his followers, oh, the utter extravagance of his work in us who trust him — endless energy, boundless strength! Ephesians 1:15b (The Message)

And I pray that you, being rooted and established in love, may have power, together with all the saints, to grasp how wide and long and high and deep is the love of Christ, and to know this

love that surpasses knowledge — that you may be filled to the measure of all the fullness of God. Ephesians 3:17b-19

God Breathes

Breathe: to inhale and exhale freely; to live

It is a scene we have seen many times - mostly on television or in the movies - a small group hovering over a limp body, perhaps performing CPR - and the only word you hear is, "Breathe! Breathe! Breathe!" Breath is the evidence of life. We serve a living God - a God who breathes. Because he is the true, living God, he alone is able to give us life, know everything about us, meet our every need, and fill us with his Spirit. He is the source of the breath of life, both physically and spiritually.

> **Psalm 33:5-6** The LORD loves righteousness and justice; the earth is full of his unfailing love. By the word of the LORD were the heavens made, their starry host by the breath of his mouth.
> **Genesis 2:7** The LORD God formed the man from the dust of the ground and breathed into his nostrils the breath of life, and the man became a living being.
> **2 Samuel 22:15-17** He shot arrows and scattered the enemies, bolts of lightning and routed them. The valleys of the sea were exposed and the foundations of the earth laid bare at the rebuke of the LORD, at

the blast of breath from his nostrils. He reached down from on high and took hold of me; he drew me out of deep waters.

2 Thessalonians 2:8 And then the lawless one will be revealed, whom the Lord Jesus will overthrow with the breath of his mouth and destroy by the splendor of his coming.

Job 32:8 But it is the spirit in a man, the breath of the Almighty, that gives him understanding.

John 20:21-22 Again Jesus said, "Peace be with you! As the Father has sent me, I am sending you." And with that he breathed on them and said, "Receive the Holy Spirit."

All Scripture is God-breathed and is useful for teaching _____, rebuking _____, correcting _____ and training _____ in righteousness. 2 Timothy 3:16

The enemy boasted, "I will pursue, I will overtake them. I will divide the spoils; I will gorge myself on them. I will draw my sword and my hand will destroy them."

But you blew with your breath, and the sea covered them. They sank like lead in the mighty waters. Who among the gods is like you, O LORD? Who is like you -majestic in holiness, awesome in glory, working wonders? Exodus 15:9-11

Let everything that has breath praise the LORD. Praise the LORD. Psalm 150:6

God Cares

Care: close attention or careful heed; to feel concern or interest in

What burden are you carrying today? It is so important as we go through life and through various trials to know that someone cares. As we look through the scriptures, we see the picture of a loving God who desires to guide us and meet our needs to the extent that he came to sacrifice himself in order to restore fellowship with us. As you read the scriptures below, focus on the God who cares for you. Worship him and give him praise for who he is, and find comfort in the truth that he cares for you.

Deuteronomy 32:9-11 For the LORD's portion is his people, Jacob his allotted inheritance. In a desert land he found him, in a barren and howling waste. He shielded him and cared for him; He guarded him as the apple of his eye, like an eagle that stirs up its nest and hovers over its young, that spreads its wings to catch them and carries them on its pinions.

Psalm 8:3-5 When I consider your heavens, the work of your fingers, the moon and the stars, which you have set in place, what is man that you are mindful of him, the son of man that you care for him? You made him a little lower than the heavenly beings and crowned him with glory and honor.

Psalm 55:16-18,22 But I call to God, and the LORD saves me. Evening, morning and noon I cry out in distress, and he hears my voice. He ransoms me unharmed from the battle waged against me, even though many oppose me. Cast your cares on the LORD and he will sustain you; he will never let the righteous fall.

Psalm 146:6-9 The Maker of heaven and earth, the sea, and everything in them — the LORD, who remains faithful forever. He upholds the cause of the oppressed and gives food to the hungry. The LORD sets prisoners free, the LORD gives sight to the blind, the LORD lifts up those who are bowed down, the LORD loves the righteous. The LORD watches over the alien and sustains the fatherless and the widow, but he frustrates the ways of the wicked.

Nahum 1:7 The LORD is good, a refuge in times of trouble. He cares for those who trust in him.

Humble yourself, therefore, _____, under God's mighty hand, that he may lift you up in due time. Cast all your anxiety on him, _____, because he cares for you. 1 Peter 5:6-7

Come, let us bow down in worship, let us kneel before the LORD our Maker; for he is our God and we are the people of his pasture, the flock under his care. Psalm 95:6-7a

God Comforts

Comfort: to encourage, help and strengthen; to console, calm or inspire with hope

Can you recall a time when you have been in distress and someone comforted you by their words or deeds? Were you encouraged? Did it give you strength and hope to endure? There are so many ways God comforts us. His word is full of inspiring accounts of those who faced extremely difficult times, yet were comforted by the word, the presence or the inspiration of God. God's word also tells us that when God comforts us, we are learning how to comfort those around us who need to be encouraged. The lesson may be difficult, but the privilege that follows is that he chooses us to comfort others as we have been comforted by him.

> **Isaiah 49:13** Shout for joy, O heavens; rejoice, O earth; burst into song, O mountains! For the Lord comforts his people and will have compassion on his afflicted ones.
> **Isaiah 51:12** I, even I, am he who comforts you. Who are you that your fear mortal men, the sons of men, who are but grass.
> **Isaiah 66:13a** As a mother comforts her child, so will I comfort you.

Psalm 23:4 Even though I walk through the valley of the shadow of death, I will fear no evil, for you are with me; your rod and your staff, they comfort me.

Psalm 119:49-50 Remember your word to your servant, for you have given me hope. My comfort in my suffering is this: Your promise preserves my life.

Psalm 119:76 May your unfailing love be my comfort, according to your promise to your servant.

Give _____ a sign of your goodness, that _____'s enemies may see it and be put to shame, for you, O LORD, have helped _____ and comforted _____. Psalm 86:17

Praise be to the God and Father of our Lord Jesus Christ, the Father of compassion and the God of all comfort who comforts us in all our troubles, so that we can comfort those in any trouble with the comfort we ourselves have received from God. For just as the sufferings of Christ flow over into our lives, so also through Christ our comfort overflows. 2 Corinthians 1:3-5

God is Compassionate

Compassion: showing loving sympathy; sorrow for the trouble of others accompanied by an urge to help

In the scriptures we see that compassion is an expression of loving sympathy followed by action. It is more than just feeling sorry. God's compassion for us has led to his forgiveness of our sin. When Jesus felt compassion, he began to teach or heal or minister to the needs of those around him. God's expression of compassion is our example of how to minister to those we encounter who are in need.

2 Kings 13:22-23 Hazael king of Aram oppressed Israel throughout the reign of Jehoahaz. But the LORD was gracious to them and had compassion and showed concern for them because of his covenant with Abraham, Isaac and Jacob. To this day he has been unwilling to destroy them or banish them from his presence.

Psalm 86:15 But you, O Lord, are a compassionate and gracious God, slow to anger, abounding in love and faithfulness.

Psalm 103:13 As a father has compassion on his children, so the LORD has compassion on those who fear him.

Psalm 116:5 The LORD is gracious and righteous; our God is full of compassion.

Psalm 145:9 The LORD is good to all; he has compassion on all he has made.

Isaiah 54:8 "In a surge of anger I hid my face from you for a moment, but with everlasting kindness I will have compassion on you," says the LORD your redeemer.

Lamentations 3:22 Because of the LORD's great love we are not consumed, for his compassions never fail.

Micah 7:19 You will again have compassion on us; you will tread our sins underfoot and hurl all our iniquities into the depths of the sea.

Mark 6:34 When Jesus landed and saw a large crowd, he had compassion on them, because they were like sheep without a shepherd. So he began teaching them many things.

Yet the LORD longs to be gracious to you, _____; He rises to show you, _____, compassion. For the LORD is a God of justice. Blessed are all who wait for him. Isaiah 30:18

Praise the LORD, O my soul; all my inmost being, praise his holy name. Praise the LORD, O my soul, and forget not all his benefits — who forgives all your sins and heals all your diseases, who redeems your life from the pit and crowns you with love and compassion, who satisfies your desires with good things so that your youth is renewed like the eagle's. Psalm 103:1-5

God Defends

Defend: to drive away danger or attack; to keep secure

How important is a strong defense? Often the picture of defense focuses on keeping the enemy away by using a wall or shield. But sometimes the attacks can come from within as well as from without. We often pray for a "hedge of protection" but forget that the hedge has thorns on both sides. That hedge protects us from ourselves as well as from the enemy. God does it all! There is no weak spot in his defense. He is our shield, our refuge, our armor, our sword - our MIGHTY defender. May it give you peace knowing that God is keeping watch.

Psalm 72:3-5 The mountains will bring prosperity to the people, the hills the fruit of righteousness. He will defend the afflicted among the people and save the children of the needy; he will crush the oppressor. He will endure as long as the sun, as long as the moon, through all generations.

Isaiah 19:20 It will be a sign and witness to the LORD Almighty in the land of Egypt. When they cry out to the LORD because of their oppressors, he will send them a savior and defender, and he will rescue them.

2 Samuel 22:31 As for God, his way is perfect; the word of the LORD is flawless. He is a shield for all who take refuge in him.

Job 1:10 Have you not put a hedge around him and his household and everything he has? You have blessed the work of his hands, so that his flocks and herds are spread throughout the land.

Ephesians 6:11 Put on the full armor of God so that you can take your stand against the devil's schemes.

Ephesians 6:17 Take the helmet of salvation and the sword of the Spirit, which is the word of God.

Blessed are you, _____. Who is like you, _____, a person saved by the Lord? He is your shield and helper and your glorious sword. Your enemies will cower before you, and you will trample down their high places. Deuteronomy 33:29

But I will defend my house against marauding forces. Never again will an oppressor overrun my people, for now I am keeping watch. Zechariah 9:8

God Encourages

Encourage: to give courage, hope or confidence; to embolden, to hearten; to give support to; be favorable to

As we read God's word throughout the Scriptures, we find encouragement in many ways. There are examples of God's power, his compassion, his wisdom and guidance. God also uses us to encourage others. Willingness to speak kind, encouraging words can be transforming. Listen to the Holy Spirit when it prompts you to greet someone with a smile and word of encouragement. It will be a blessing to them and it will bless you as you serve him by encouraging others.

God encourages - **Psalm 10:17-18** You hear, O LORD, the desire of the afflicted; you encourage them, and you listen to their cry, defending the fatherless and the oppressed, in order that man, who is of the earth, may terrify no more.

God's Word encourages – **Romans 15:4** For everything that was written in the past was written to teach us, so that through endurance and the encouragement of the Scriptures we might have hope.

God's gift to us – **Romans 12:6-8** We have different gifts, according to the grace given us. If a man's gift is prophesying, let him use it in proportion to his faith. If it is serving, let him serve; if it is teaching, let him teach; if it is encouraging, let him encourage; if it is contributing to the needs of others, let him give generously; if it is leadership, let him govern diligently; if it is showing mercy, let him do it cheerfully.

God's model of encouragement – **Colossians 2:2-3** My purpose is that they may be encouraged in heart and united in love, so that they may have the full riches of complete understanding, in order that they may know the mystery of God, namely, Christ, in whom are hidden all the treasures of wisdom and knowledge.

God's command to us – **Ephesians 4:29** Do not let any unwholesome talk come out of your mouths, but only what is helpful for building others up according to their needs, that it may benefit those who listen.

Hebrews 3:13 But encourage one another daily, as long as it is called Today, so that none of you may be hardened by sin's deceitfulness.

May our Lord Jesus Christ himself and God our Father, who loved _____ and by his grace gave _____ eternal encouragement and good hope, encourage _____'s heart and strengthen _____ in every good deed and word. 2 Thessalonians 2:16-17

If you have any encouragement from being united with Christ, if any comfort from his love, if any fellowship with the Spirit, if any tenderness and compassion, then make my joy complete by being like-minded, having the same love, being one in spirit and purpose. Philippians 2:1-2

God Endures

Endure: to undergo without giving in; to regard with acceptance or tolerance; to continue in the same state; to remain firm under suffering or misfortune without yielding

When I think of endurance, I recall the image of Olympic athletes. Although they test the limits of their bodies and suffer exhaustion and pain, they continue to press on toward the prize. When I consider the endurance of God, I recall a scene in a motion picture that depicts the beating that Jesus endured before he was crucified. The scene was gruesome and it seemed to go on and on. I found myself yearning for it to stop and asking myself how he was able to endure such pain and suffering. In the scriptures it tells us that Jesus was also considering the prize. His love for you and for me is so strong, and his desire to redeem us so great that he was willing to endure the suffering and pain. Incredibly, the joy set before him was the hope of a personal relationship with you and me. The scriptures tell us about his enduring love and faithfulness from generation to generation. How amazing – his love endures forever!

1 Chronicles 16:34 Give thanks to the LORD, for he is good; His love endures forever.

Psalm 100:5 For the LORD is good and his love endures forever; His faithfulness continues through all generations.

Psalm 102:11-12 My days are like the evening shadow; I wither away like grass. But you, O LORD, sit enthroned forever; your renown endures through all generations.

Psalm 111:2-3 Great are the works of the LORD; they are pondered by all who delight in them. Glorious and majestic are his deeds, and his righteousness endures forever.

Psalm 117:2 For great is his love toward us, and the faithfulness of the LORD endures forever. Praise the LORD.

Psalm 119:90-91 Your faithfulness continues through all generations; you established the earth, and it endures. Your laws endure to this day, for all things serve you.

Psalm 135:13 Your name, O LORD, endures forever, your renown, O LORD, through all generations.

Psalm 145:13 Your kingdom is an everlasting kingdom, and your dominion endures through all generations. The LORD is faithful to all his promises and loving toward all he has made.

Ecclesiastes 3:14 I know that everything God does will endure forever; nothing can be added to it and nothing taken from it. God does it so that men will revere him.

_____, *Consider him who endured such opposition from sinful men, so that you, _____, will not grow weary and lose heart. Hebrews 12:3*

Let us fix our eyes on Jesus, the author and perfecter of our faith, who for the joy set before him endured the cross, scorning its shame, and sat down at the right hand of the throne of God.

Hebrews 12:2

God Equips

Equip: to furnish for service or action by appropriate provisioning; to make ready

Every day we are faced with situations for which we may have little or no experience or training. It is easy to give in to doubt or despair if we think we are alone in such a situation. In **Philippians 4:13** the scripture tells us, "I can do all things through Christ who strengthens me." and in **verse 19**, "And my God will supply all your needs according to his riches in glory in Christ Jesus." We are never alone. Through Christ, we are strong and fully equipped. We must focus on how God equips us, and then we are able to face each situation with confidence.

Physical attributes - **Proverbs 20:12** Ears that hear and eyes that see — the LORD has made them both.

Training - **Exodus 4:10-12** Moses said to the LORD, "O Lord, I have never been eloquent, neither in the past nor since you have spoken to your servant. I am slow of speech and tongue." The LORD said to him, "Who gave man his mouth? Who makes him deaf or mute? Who gives him sight or makes him blind? Is it not I, the LORD? Now go; I will help you speak and will teach you what to say."

Written instructions and guidance - **2 Timothy 3:16-17** All Scripture is God-breathed and is useful for teaching, rebuking, correcting and training in righteousness, so that the man of God may be thoroughly equipped for every good work.

God given power and all that we need - **Matthew 10:8-10** Jesus sent his twelve harvest hands out with this charge: Don't begin by traveling to some far-off place to convert unbelievers. And don't try to be dramatic by tackling some public enemy. Go to the lost, confused people right here in the neighborhood. Tell them that the kingdom is here. Bring health to the sick. Raise the dead. Touch the untouchables. Kick out the demons. You have been treated generously, so live generously. Don't think you have to put on a fund-raising campaign before you start. You don't need a lot of equipment. You are the equipment, and all you need to keep that going is three meals a day. Travel light. (The Message)

Understanding and power - **Luke 24:45-49** Then he opened their minds so they could understand the Scriptures. He told them, "This is what is written: The Christ will suffer and rise from the dead on the third day, and repentance and forgiveness of sins will be preached in his name to all nations, beginning at Jerusalem. You are witnesses of these things. I am going to send you what my Father has promised; but stay in the city until you have been clothed (equipped) with power from on high."

Grace to bring others to Christ - **Ephesians 3:7-8** This is my life work: helping people understand and respond to this Message. It came as a sheer gift to me, a real surprise, God handling all the details.

When it came to presenting the Message to people who had no background in God's way, I was the least qualified of any of the available Christians. God saw to it that I was equipped, but you can be sure that it had nothing to do with my natural abilities. (The Message)

May the God of peace... equip you, _____, with every-thing good for doing his will, and may he work in _____ what is pleasing to him, through Jesus Christ, to whom be glory for ever and ever. Amen. Hebrews 13:20a,21

Finally, be strong in the Lord and in his mighty <u>power</u>. Put on the full armor of God so that you can take your stand against the devil's schemes. For our struggle is not against flesh and blood, but against the rulers, against the authorities, against the powers of this dark world and against the spiritual forces of evil in the heavenly realms. Therefore put on the full armor of God, so that when the day of evil comes, you may be able to stand your ground, and after you have done every-thing, to stand. Stand firm then, with the belt of <u>truth</u> buckled around your waist, with the breast-plate of <u>righteousness</u> in place, and with your feet fitted with the <u>readiness</u> that comes from the <u>gospel of peace</u>. In addition to all this, take up the shield of <u>faith</u>, with which you can extinguish all the flaming arrows of the evil one. Take the helmet of <u>salvation</u> and the sword of the Spirit, which is the <u>word of God</u>. And pray in the Spirit on all occasions with all kinds of prayers and requests. With this in mind, be alert and always keep on praying for all the saints. Ephesians 6:10-18

God is Exact / Precise

Exact: marked by strict, particular and complete accordance with fact or standard; thorough consideration or minute measurement of small factual details

Precise: exactly or sharply defined or stated; minutely exact

God has an exact nature. By some this might be considered "narrow-minded," however, one can also see it as God's specific message through his word to assure that we know the path to the salvation he offers. The scriptures show his exact nature from the Old Testament through the New Testament. Jesus says, "I am <u>the way, the truth and the life.</u> The enemy would like to confuse that message with alternative paths, yet God's word is exact and he clearly shows us how to establish fellowship with him. God knows you specifically, right down to the number of hairs on your head, and he has exact plans for you. His plans are precise and perfect.

Genesis 7:1-5 The LORD then said to Noah, "Go into the ark, you and your whole family, because I have found you righteous in this generation. Take with you seven of every kind of clean animal, a male and its mate, and two of every kind of unclean animal, a male and its mate, and also seven of every kind of bird, male and female, to keep their various kinds alive throughout the earth. Seven days from now I will send rain on the earth for forty days and forty nights, and I will wipe from the face of the earth every living creature I have made." And Noah did all that the LORD commanded him.

Exodus 25:8-9 Then have them make a sanctuary for me, and I will dwell among them. Make this tabernacle and all its furnishings exactly like the pattern I will show you.

Psalm 139:13-16 Oh yes, you shaped me first inside, then out; you formed me in my mother's womb. I thank you, High God — you're breathtaking! Body and soul, I am marvelously made! I worship in adoration — what a creation! You know me inside and out, you know every bone in my body; you know exactly how I was made, bit-by-bit, how I was sculpted from nothing into something. Like an open book, you watched me grow from conception to birth; all the stages of my life were spread out before you, the days of my life all prepared before I'd even lived one day.

Matthew 10:29-31a Are not two sparrows sold for a penny? Yet not one of them will fall to the ground apart from the will of your Father. And even the very hairs of your head are all numbered.

John 14:30-31 I will not speak with you much longer, for the prince of this world is coming. He has no hold on me, but the world must learn that I love the Father and that I do exactly what my Father has commanded me.

John 14:6 Jesus answered, "I am the way and the truth and the life. No one comes to the Father except through me."

Acts 17:25-27 And he is not served by human hands, as if he needed anything, because he himself gives all men life and breath and everything else. From one man he made every nation of men, that they should inhabit the whole earth; and he determined the times set for them and the exact places where they should live. God did this so that men would seek him and perhaps reach out for him and find him, though he is not far from each one of us.

Hebrews 1:3 The Son is the radiance of God's glory and the exact representation of his being, sustaining all things by his powerful word. After he had provided purification for sins, he sat down at the right hand of the Majesty in heaven.

*So be very careful, _____, to act exactly as G*O*D commands you. Don't veer off to the right or the left. Walk straight down the road G*O*D commands so that you, ____ ___, will have a good life and live a long time in the land that you're about to possess. Deuteronomy 5:32-33 (The Message)*

Everyone has to die once, then face the consequences. Christ's death was also a one-time event, but it was a sacrifice that took care of sins forever. And so, when he next appears, the outcome for those eager to greet him is, precisely, salvation. Hebrews 9:27-28 (The Message)

.

God is Faithful

Faithful: worthy of trust; consistently reliable

One of the verses I memorized as a new Christian was 1 Corinthians 10:13 "No temptation has seized you except what is common to man. And God is faithful; he will not let you be tempted beyond what you can bear. But when you are tempted, he will also provide a way out so that you can stand up under it." The phrase that always stands out to me is "God is faithful." In each and every situation, God is faithful. He is reliable and trustworthy. Another verse, **Deuteronomy 31:8 states**, "The LORD himself goes before you and will be with you; he will never leave you nor forsake you. Do not be afraid; do not be discouraged." The faithfulness of God is shown throughout the scriptures. God is faithful and worthy of our trust.

Exodus 34:5-6 Then the LORD came down in the cloud and stood there with him and proclaimed his name, the LORD. And he passed in front of Moses, proclaiming, "The LORD, the LORD, the compassionate and gracious God, slow to anger, abounding in love and faithfulness."

Deuteronomy 7:9 Know therefore that the LORD your God is God; he is the faithful God, keeping his covenant of love to a thousand generations of those who love him and keep his commands.

Deuteronomy 32:4 He is the Rock, his works are perfect, and all his ways are just. A faithful God who does no wrong, upright and just is he.

Psalm 33:4 For the word of the LORD is right and true; he is faithful in all he does.

Psalm 36:5 Your love, O LORD, reaches to the heavens, your faithfulness to the skies.

Psalm 86:15 But you, O Lord, are a compassionate and gracious God, slow to anger, abounding in love and faithfulness.

Psalm 145:13 Your kingdom is an everlasting kingdom, and your dominion endures through all generations. The LORD is faithful to all his promises and loving toward all he has made.

Lamentations 3:22-23 Because of the Lord's great love we are not consumed, for his compassions never fail. They are new every morning; great is your faithfulness.

But the Lord is faithful, and he will strengthen and protect you, _____, from the evil one. May the Lord direct your heart, _____, into God's love and Christ's perseverance. 2 Thessalonians 3:3,5

O LORD God Almighty, who is like you? You are mighty, O LORD, and your faithfulness surrounds you. **Psalm 89:8**

Not to us, O LORD, not to us but to your name be the glory, because of your love and faithfulness. **Psalm 115:1**

God says "Fear Not"

Fear: a feeling of anxiety, uneasiness or apprehension by the presence or nearness of danger, evil, or pain

In the Bible, one of the first accounts of fear is found in **Genesis 3:10** when God called out to Adam after he and Eve had eaten the forbidden fruit. Adam responded to God's call saying, "I heard you in the garden, and I was afraid." At that moment, the joy and fellowship that Adam had experienced with God turned to fear. Yet God did not want fear to be the nature of our relationship. His love for us set in motion the plan to restore that joyful fellowship that he intended from the beginning of creation.

Now fast forward to the time of the birth of Jesus. Imagine that night, as the shepherds cared for their flocks in the hills around Bethlehem when suddenly the skies were filled with angels. The shepherds were terrified and fearful! Yet the clear message from God spoken by the angelic chorus was, "Fear not!" In his love, God sent Jesus, our Savior, to restore the fellowship that was broken. Love is the opposite of fear. As stated in **1 John 4:18**, "There is no fear in love. But perfect love drives out fear..." As you focus on God's perfect love, that declaration continues to ring out to each of us in any moment that we are fearful. Fear not!

Isaiah 41:13 For I am the LORD, your God, who takes hold of your right hand and says to you, Do not fear; I will help you.

Isaiah 43:1 But now, this is what the LORD says — he who created you, O Jacob, he who formed you, O Israel: "Fear not, for I have redeemed you; I have summoned you by name; you are mine."

Isaiah 51:7 Hear me, you who know what is right, you people who have my law in your hearts: Do not fear the reproach of men or be terrified by their insults.

Isaiah 54:14 In righteousness you will be established: Tyranny will be far from you; you will have nothing to fear. Terror will be far removed; it will not come near you.

Luke 2:8-11 And there were shepherds living out in the fields nearby, keeping watch over their flocks at night. An angel of the Lord appeared to them, and the glory of the Lord shone around them, and they were terrified. But the angel said to them, "Do not be afraid. I bring you good news of great joy that will be for all the people. Today in the town of David a Savior has been born to you; he is Christ the Lord.

Lamentations 3:57 You came near when I called you, and you said, "Do not fear."

So do not fear, _____, for I am with you; do not be dismayed, _____, for am your God. I will strengthen you and help you, _____; I will uphold you with my righteous right hand. Isaiah 41:10

The Lord is my light and my salvation - whom shall I fear? The Lord is the stronghold of my life - of whom shall I be afraid? Psalm 27:1

God Fills

Fill: to put into as much as can be held or contained; to supply with a full complement; to satisfy

Have you ever experienced a time when you felt empty? It is during these times that we must look to God to fill us. As the scriptures tell us, God is able to fill us with laughter and joy. He will satisfy our hunger and thirst. His presence fills the universe and he fills us with the Holy Spirit. When we are filled with him, all the emptiness is satisfied and we are able to see his glory. If you are empty, go to God and be filled.

Exodus 40:34-35 Then the cloud covered the Tent of Meeting, and the glory of the LORD filled the tabernacle. Moses could not enter the Tent of Meeting because the cloud had settled upon it, and the glory of the LORD filled the tabernacle.

Job 8:20-22 Surely God does not reject a blameless man or strengthen the hands of evildoers. He will yet fill your mouth with laughter and your lips with shouts of joy.

Psalm 4:6-8 Many are asking, "Who can show us any good?" Let the light of your face shine upon us, O LORD. You have filled my heart with greater joy than when their grain and new wine abound. I will lie down and sleep in peace, for you alone, O LORD, make me dwell in safety.

Psalm 16:11 You have made known to me the path of life; you will fill me with joy in your presence, with eternal pleasures at your right hand.

Psalm 107:8-9 Let them give thanks to the LORD for his unfailing love and his wonderful deeds for men, for he satisfies the thirsty and fills the hungry with good things.

Jeremiah 23:23-25 "Am I only a God nearby," declares the LORD, "and not a God far away? Can anyone hide in secret places so that I cannot see him?" declares the LORD. "Do not I fill heaven and earth?" declares the LORD.

Matthew 5:6 Blessed are those who hunger and thirst for righteousness, for they will be filled.

...may you, _____, have power, together with all the saints, to grasp how wide and long and high and deep is the love of Christ, and to know this love that surpasses knowledge — that you, _____, may be filled to the measure of all the fullness of God. Ephesians 3:18-19

After they prayed, the place where they were meeting was shaken. And they were all filled with the Holy Spirit and spoke the word of God boldly. Acts 4:31

God is our Focus

Focus: to adjust in order to produce a clear image; to fix or settle on one thing; to concentrate

In order to know someone – to really know them well – to know them in such a way that you fully trust them and have confidence in their character, requires periods of time when you fully focus on that person. As you spend time with them you are able to observe their actions. You see how they respond to various situations. You watch them as they interact with others and listen to their words. In time, you are able to see the attributes possessed by this person and determine the nature of your relationship.

The way we "see God" is to read about him in the scriptures. As we learn about his nature, the more intimate our relationship becomes, and the more we can put our faith and trust in him. I am learning to fully focus on God when I pray. Rather than focus on my situation or my need, I focus on God and his nature. As I consider his attributes, I realize that I am not alone and that God listens to my prayer and will respond as only he can to meet my need.

The scriptures show many examples of those who kept their focus on God rather than their circumstances. In each situation, God was and is faithful. Keeping God fully in focus is the key to peace and victorious living.

Genesis 6:11-14,17-19,22 Now the earth was corrupt in God's sight and was full of violence. God saw how corrupt the earth had become, for all the people on earth had corrupted their ways. So God said to Noah, "I am going to put an end to all people, for the earth is filled with violence because of them. I am surely going to destroy both them and the earth. So make yourself an ark of cypress wood; make rooms in it and coat it with pitch inside and out. I am going to bring floodwaters on the earth to destroy all life under the heavens, every creature that has the breath of life in it. Everything on earth will perish. But I will establish my covenant with you, and you will enter the ark — you and your sons and your wife and your sons' wives with you. You are to bring into the ark two of all living creatures, male and female, to keep them alive with you." Noah did everything just as God commanded him.

Genesis 22:6-8 Abraham took the wood for the burnt offering and placed it on his son Isaac, and he himself carried the fire and the knife. As the two of them went on together, Isaac spoke up and said to his father Abraham, "Father?" "Yes, my son?" Abraham replied. "The fire and wood are here," Isaac said, "but where is the lamb for the burnt offering?" Abraham answered, "God himself will provide the lamb for the burnt offering, my son." And the two of them went on together.

1 Samuel 17:45-47 David said to the Philistine, "You come against me with sword and spear and javelin, but I come against you in the name of the LORD Almighty, the God of the armies of Israel, whom you have defied. This day the LORD will hand you over to me, and I'll strike you down and cut off your head. Today I will give the carcasses of the

Philistine army to the birds of the air and the beasts of the earth, and the whole world will know that there is a God in Israel. All those gathered here will know that it is not by sword or spear that the LORD saves; for the battle is the LORD's, and he will give all of you into our hands."

Daniel 3:16-17 Shadrach, Meshach and Abednego replied to the king, "O Nebuchadnezzar, we do not need to defend ourselves before you in this matter. If we are thrown into the blazing furnace, the God we serve is able to save us from it, and he will rescue us from your hand, O king.

Proverbs 3:5-6 Trust in the LORD with all your heart and lean not on your own understanding; in all your ways acknowledge (focus on) him, and he will make your paths straight.

Here's what I want you to do, _____: Find a quiet, secluded place so you won't be tempted to role-play before God. Just be there as simply and honestly as you can manage. The focus will shift from you, _____, to God, and you, _____, will begin to sense his grace. Matthew 6:6 (The Message)

You will keep in perfect peace all who trust in you, all whose thoughts are fixed (focused) on you! Isaiah 26:3 (New Living Translation)

God Forgives

Forgive: to grant relief from payment; to pardon

*I*n Old Testament times specific actions were required to receive forgiveness for sin.*

Leviticus 4:27-31 If a member of the community sins unintentionally and does what is forbidden in any of the LORD's commands, he is guilty. When he is made aware of the sin he committed, he must bring as his offering for the sin he committed a female goat without defect. He is to lay his hand on the head of the sin offering and slaughter it at the place of the burnt offering. Then the priest is to take some of the blood with his finger and put it on the horns of the altar of burnt offering and pour out the rest of the blood at the base of the altar. He shall remove all the fat, just as the fat is removed from the fellowship offering, and the priest shall burn it on the altar as an aroma pleasing to the LORD. In this way the priest will make atonement for him, and he will be forgiven.

Under the New Covenant we are cleansed by the sacrificial blood of Jesus.

Matthew 26:28 This is my blood of the covenant, which is poured out for many for the forgiveness of sins.

So that now, we need only to confess our sin to be forgiven.

1 John 1:9 If we confess our sins, he is faithful and just and will forgive us our sins and purify us from all unrighteousness.

But sometimes it is easier to feel guilty than to ask forgiveness.

It is hard to comprehend how a Holy God can forget our sin as a result of a simple, yet sincere confession. Our guilt overwhelms us and we find it hard to confess. This was shown to me so clearly recently as my granddaughter, tearful and in agony, knowing that she had done something wrong, cried out, "I can't say I'm sorry! I can't! It's too hard."

Yet there is no sin so great, that the blood of Jesus is not sufficient to wash our soul clean. We must only be obedient to confess it to him. Then we must receive the forgiveness that he freely offers. When forgiven, we must choose to take off the cloak of guilt that the enemy would have us wear and rejoice in the newness of life that we receive. The result is healing and an overwhelming love and gratitude to the one who forgives.

Psalm 130:3-5 If you, O LORD, kept a record of sins, O Lord, who could stand? But with you there is forgiveness; therefore you are feared. I wait for the LORD, my soul waits, and in his word I put my hope.

Micah 7:18-19 Who is a God like you, who pardons sin and forgives the transgression of the remnant of his inheritance? You do not stay angry forever but delight to show mercy. You will again have compassion on us; you will tread our sins underfoot and hurl all our iniquities into the depths of the sea.

Colossians 1:13-14 For he has rescued us from the dominion of darkness and brought us into the kingdom of the son he loves, in whom we have redemption, the forgiveness of sins.

Acts 13:38-39 Therefore, my brothers, I want you to know that through Jesus the forgiveness of sins is proclaimed to you. Through him everyone who believes is justified from everything you could not be justified from by the law of Moses.

...open _____'s eyes and turn _____ from darkness to light, and from the power of Satan to God, so that _____ may receive forgiveness of sins and a place among those who are sanctified by faith ... Acts 26:18-19

...if my people, who are called by my name, will humble themselves and pray and seek my face and turn from their wicked ways, then will I hear from heaven and will forgive their sin and will heal their land. 2 Chronicles 7:14

God Forms the Mold

Form: to shape or mold into a certain state after a particular model

Mold: distinctive nature or character; to determine or influence the quality or nature of

"Why did God make me this way?" That might be one of the most frequent questions ever asked. Yet, when we consider that we are the creation of God, whose wisdom is beyond anything we can imagine, the answer to that question directs us to the possibility of purpose. God makes no mistakes, and when he formed your mold — physically, emotionally, mentally — his plan and purpose for you as an individual was to bring glory to him. Rest in the knowledge that the Master Potter formed the mold that became you, and in his plan, you are uniquely perfect.

> **Genesis 2:7** The LORD God formed the man from the dust of the ground and breathed into his nostrils the breath of life, and the man became a living being.
> **Psalm 33:13-15** From heaven the Lord looks down and sees all mankind; from his dwelling place

he watches all who live on earth — he who forms the hearts of all, who considers everything they do.

Psalm 103:13-14 As a father has compassion on his children, so the LORD has compassion on those who fear him; for he knows how we are formed, he remembers that we are dust.

Romans 9:20-21 But who are you, O man, to talk back to God? Shall what is formed say to him who formed it, "Why did you make me like this?" Does not the potter have the right to make out of the same lump of clay some pottery for noble purposes and some for common use?

Isaiah 64:8 Yet, O LORD, you are our Father. We are the clay, you are the potter; we are all the work of your hand.

Isaiah 43:5-7 Do not be afraid, for I am with you; I will bring your children from the east and gather you from the west. I will say to the north, "Give them up!" and to the south, "Do not hold them back." Bring my sons from afar and my daughters from the ends of the earth — everyone who is called by my name, whom I created for my glory, whom I formed and made.

Your hands made _____ and formed _____; give _ _____ understanding to learn your commands. May those who fear you rejoice when they see _____, for (he/she) has put (his/her) hope in your word. Psalm 119:73-74

As you do not know the path of the wind, or how the body is formed in a mother's womb, so you cannot understand the work of God, the maker of all things. Ecclesiastes 11:5-6

God Gives Freedom

Freedom: not bound, confined or detained by force; liberation from the power of another

If God were subject to any other person, force or thing, he would not be free and could not impart freedom. Because he is totally free, he is the source of freedom. That freedom brings many facets to our lives and allows us to enjoy a freedom like no other. He alone is able to break the bonds of the enemy. When I am in him, I am no longer bound by forces that would enslave me. I am free!

    Psalm 118:4-5 Let those who fear the LORD say: "His love endures forever." In my anguish I cried to the LORD, and he answered by setting me free.
    Psalm 119:32 I run in the path of your commands, for you have set my heart free.
    John 8:32 Then you will know the truth, and the truth will set you free.
    John 8:36 So if the Son sets you free, you will be free indeed.
    Romans 8:1-2 Therefore, there is now no condemnation for those who are in Christ Jesus because through Christ Jesus the law of the Spirit of life set me free from the law of sin and death.

James 1:25 But the man who looks intently into the perfect law that gives freedom, and continues to do this, not forgetting what he has heard, but doing it — he will be blessed in what he does.

It is for freedom that Christ has set you, _____, free. Stand firm, then, _____, and do not let yourself be burdened again by a yoke of slavery. Galatians 5:1

The Spirit of the Sovereign LORD is on me, because the LORD has anointed me to preach good news to the poor. He has sent me to bind up the brokenhearted, to proclaim freedom for the captives and release from darkness for the prisoners. Isaiah 61:1

God Gives

Give: to grant, bestow or provide; to yield or produce

One line in a hymn says, "…For out of his infinite riches in Jesus, he giveth, and giveth, and giveth again." Read these verses that begin to illustrate God's giving nature. Then just read the bold type in each verse. As you read them, one after another, it becomes clear that God gives to us abundantly and provides for all our needs. He gives — we receive.

Isaiah 42:5 This is what God the LORD says — he who created the heavens and stretched them out, who spread out the earth and all that comes out of it, **who gives breath to its people, and life to those who walk on it.**

Genesis 9: 3 Everything that lives and moves will be food for you. **Just as I gave you the green plants, I now give you everything.**

Jeremiah 5:24b Let us fear the LORD our God, who **gives autumn and spring rains in season,** who assures us of the regular weeks of harvest.

Genesis 27:20 Isaac asked his son, "How did you find it so quickly, my son?" **"The LORD your God gave me success,"** he replied.

Joshua 22:3 For a long time now — to this very day — you have not deserted your brothers but have carried out the **mission the LORD your God gave you.**

Joshua 23:14 Now I am about to go the way of all the earth. You know with all your heart and soul that not one of all the **good promises the LORD your God gave you** has failed. Every promise has been fulfilled; not one has failed.

2 Chronicles 15:15 All Judah rejoiced about the oath because they had sworn it wholeheartedly. They sought God eagerly, and he was found by them. **So the LORD gave them rest** on every side.

Psalm 94: 17 Unless the LORD had **given me help**, I would soon have dwelt in the silence of death.

Daniel 1:17 To these four young men **God gave knowledge and understanding** of all kinds of literature and learning. And Daniel could understand visions and dreams of all kinds.

John 3:16 For God so loved the world that **he gave his one and only Son**, that whoever believes in him shall not perish but have eternal life.

John 6:33 For the bread of God is he who comes down from heaven and **gives life to the world.**

John 3:34 For the one whom God has sent speaks the words of God, for **God gives the Spirit without limit.**

1 Corinthians: 15:57 But thanks be to God! **He gives us the victory** through our Lord Jesus Christ.

2 Thessalonians 2:16-17 May our Lord Jesus Christ himself and God our Father, who loved us and by his grace **gave us eternal encouragement and good hope**, encourage your hearts and strengthen you in every good deed and word.

Romans 4:17b ...the God who **gives life to the dead** and calls things that are not as though they were.

Romans 15:5 May the **God who gives endurance and encouragement** give you a spirit of unity among yourselves as you follow Christ Jesus.

James 1:5 If any of you lacks **wisdom**, he should ask **God, who gives generously** to all without finding fault, and it will be given to him.

Revelation 21:23 The city does not need the sun or the moon to shine on it, for the **glory of God gives it light,** and the Lamb is its lamp.

Give and it will be given to you, _____. A good measure, pressed down, shaken together and running over, will be poured into your lap. For with the measure you use, _____, it will be measured to you. Luke 6:38

God opposes the proud but gives grace to the humble. Humble yourself, therefore, under God's mighty hand, that he may lift you up in due time. Cast all your anxiety on him because he cares for you. 1 Peter 5:5b,6,7

God is Glorious

Glorious: full of glory (splendor, radiant beauty, magnificence); illustrious; giving or bringing glory

God is glorious. There are times when the beauty of nature causes me to pause. I see the beautiful green of the trees, the colorful flowers, the clear blue sky. I am filled with wonder and gratitude for God's creative works and I see his glory. There are times when I ponder the vastness of space, the stability of the universe, the wonders of the earth; its oceans, mountains and desserts, and again, I see God's glory. When I look into the face of a child and consider how the body is formed and grows and functions so perfectly, I see God's glory. If what we see now reflects his glory, what must heaven be like? Because of his glorious grace, we have the opportunity to experience his glory.

1 Chronicles 29:12-13 Wealth and honor come from you; you are the ruler of all things. In your hands are strength and power to exalt and give strength to all. Now, our God, we give you thanks, and praise your glorious name.

Psalm 66:2 Sing the glory of his name; make his praise glorious!

Psalm 72:19 Praise be to his glorious name forever; may the whole earth be filled with his glory. Amen and Amen.

Psalm 111:2-4 Great are the works of the LORD; they are pondered by all who delight in them. Glorious and majestic are his deeds, and his righteousness endures forever. He has caused his wonders to be remembered; the LORD is gracious and compassionate.

Psalm 145:4-6 One generation will commend your works to another; they will tell of your mighty acts. They will speak of the glorious splendor of your majesty, and I will meditate on your wonderful works. They will tell of the power of your awesome works, and I will proclaim your great deeds.

Psalm 145:11-13 They will tell of the glory of your kingdom and speak of your might, so that all men may know of your mighty acts and the glorious splendor of your kingdom. Your kingdom is an everlasting kingdom, and your dominion endures through all generations. The LORD is faithful to all his promises and loving toward all he has made.

Isaiah 12:5 Sing to the LORD, for he has done glorious things; let this be known to all the world.

Ephesians 1:6 To the praise of his glorious grace, which he has freely given us in the One he loves.

I keep asking that the God of our Lord Jesus Christ, the glorious Father, may give you, _____, the Spirit of wisdom and revelation, so that you, _____, may know him better. Ephesians 1:17

To him who is able to keep you from falling and to present you before his glorious presence without fault and with great joy — to the only God our

Savior be glory, majesty, power and authority, through Jesus Christ our Lord, before all ages, now and forevermore! Amen. Jude 1:24-25

God is Good

Good: honorable, worthy, dependable, reliable, right, thorough, complete, sufficient

God is good. In a world that has a measure of evil, there are many who question God's goodness. Yet, when we focus on good things, we see that they all come from God. If you read the list of God's attributes in this book, it is easy to see that God is good. That is important to know and to focus on as we pray, for we know that because he is good, we can trust that his plans for us are good. If you have not experienced his goodness, as the scripture says, "Taste and see that the Lord is good." How do we "taste" him? Take time to fully focus on him. His goodness will be evident and sweet.

Exodus 33:19 And the LORD said, "I will cause all my goodness to pass in front of you, and I will proclaim my name, the LORD, in your presence. I will have mercy on whom I will have mercy, and I will have compassion on whom I will have compassion."

1 Chronicles 16:34 Give thanks to the LORD, for he is good; his love endures forever.

Nehemiah 9:13 You came down on Mount Sinai; you spoke to them from heaven. You gave them regulations and laws that are just and right, and decrees and commands that are good.

Psalm 25:7 Remember not the sins of my youth and my rebellious ways; according to your love remember me, for you are good, O LORD.

Psalm 31:19 How great is your goodness, which you have stored up for those who fear you, which you bestow in the sight of men on those who take refuge in you.

Psalm 34:8 Taste and see that the LORD is good; blessed is the man who takes refuge in him.

Psalm 86:5 You are forgiving and good, O Lord, abounding in love to all who call to you.

Psalm 107: 8-9 Let them give thanks to the LORD for his unfailing love and his wonderful deeds for men, for he satisfies the thirsty and fills the hungry with good things.

Psalm 145:9 The LORD is good to all; he has compassion on all he has made.

Nahum 1:7 The LORD is good, a refuge in times of trouble. He cares for those who trust in him.

John 10:11 I am the good shepherd. The good shepherd lays down his life for the sheep.

Teach _____ to do your will, for you are _____'s God; may your good Spirit lead _____ on level ground. Psalm 119:68

Every good and perfect gift is from above, coming down from the Father of the heavenly lights, who does not change like shifting shadows. James 1:17

God is our Guide

Guide: the act or process of giving direction

When I go on a trip, visiting a place I have never been, there are several methods I use to find my way around. I rely on maps, pamphlets, the Internet, advice from those who have been there or who live there, and even the GPS devices. Yet, even with all of these tools available, still I get lost at one time or another. I always enjoy the guided tours, because I can relax and enjoy the trip, knowing that I will get the most out of my trip and not lose my way.

The scriptures paint a picture of God as a guide who is loving, trustworthy, and protective. He is gentle and humble, making sure that we are walking in the right path that leads to truth. This journey of life is filled with hope with God as my guide and he never leaves my side.

> **Exodus 15:13** In your unfailing love you will lead the people you have redeemed. In your strength you will guide them to your holy dwelling.
>
> **Psalm 23:2-3** He makes me lie down in green pastures, he leads me beside quiet waters, he restores my soul. He guides me in paths of righteousness for his name's sake.

Psalm 25:8-9 Good and upright is the LORD; therefore he instructs sinners in his ways. He guides the humble in what is right and teaches them his way.

Psalm 32:8 I will instruct you and teach you in the way you should go; I will counsel you and watch over you.

Isaiah 58:11 The LORD will guide you always; he will satisfy your needs in a sun-scorched land and will strengthen your frame. You will be like a well-watered garden, like a spring whose waters never fail.

John 16:13 But when he, the Spirit of truth, comes, he will guide you into all truth. He will not speak on his own; he will speak only what he hears, and he will tell you what is yet to come.

Show _____ your ways, O Lord, teach _____ your paths; guide _____ in your truth and teach _____, for you are God _____'s Savior, and _____'s hope is in you all day long. Psalm 25:4-5

Walk about Zion, go around her, count her towers, consider well her ramparts, view her citadels, that you may tell of them to the next generation. For this God is our God for ever and ever; He will be our guide even to the end. Psalm 48:12-14

God Heals

Heal: to make sound, well or healthy again; to restore; to free from grief, troubles, or evil; to reconcile; to be cured

There are many ways that we need to be healed. God alone is able to heal completely and in every way. His method of healing and his timing are perfect. When we are fully focused on him, though our bodies may be failing, our spirit remains strong. At times we ask why we must endure suffering, but God does not make us sick, he makes us well. As we catch a glimpse of his glory, God heals.

> **Exodus 15:26** He said, "If you listen carefully to the voice of the LORD your God and do what is right in his eyes, if you pay attention to his commands and keep all his decrees, I will not bring on you any of the diseases I brought on the Egyptians, for I am the LORD, who heals you."
>
> **2 Kings 20:5** Go back and tell Hezekiah, the leader of my people, "This is what the LORD, the God of your father David, says: I have heard your prayer and seen your tears; I will heal you. On the third day from now you will go up to the temple of the LORD."

Psalm 30:2 O LORD my God, I called to you for help and you healed me.

Psalm 103:2-3 Praise the LORD, O my soul, and forget not all his benefits — who forgives all your sins and heals all your diseases.

Psalm 147:3 He heals the brokenhearted and binds up their wounds.

Jeremiah 17:14 Heal me, O LORD, and I will be healed; save me and I will be saved, for you are the one I praise.

Luke 4:40 When the sun was setting, the people brought to Jesus all who had various kinds of sickness, and laying his hands on each one, he healed them.

But he was pierced for _____'s transgressions, he was crushed for _____'s iniquities; the punishment that brought _____ peace was upon him, and by his wounds _____ is healed. Isaiah 53:5

...if my people, who are called by my name, will humble themselves and pray and seek my face and turn from their wicked ways, then will I hear from heaven and will forgive their sin and will heal their land. 2 Chronicles 7:14

Therefore confess your sins to each other and pray for each other so that you may be healed. The prayer of a righteous man is powerful and effective. James 5:16

God Helps

Help: to give assistance or support; to give relief to

Help! That one word is the word we use to summon assistance when we see that our abilities are insufficient to meet the situation we face. God hears that one word prayer. He is present. He is ready and able to help, no matter how large or how small the need. I have found that helping others results in a good feeling that encourages a continued desire to help those in need. Our God is ready, able and eager to help. I believe his desire is to help us more and more. We must only cry out to him. Help!

> **2 Chronicles 14:11** Then Asa called to the LORD his God and said, "LORD, there is no one like you to help the powerless against the mighty. Help us, O LORD our God, for we rely on you, and in your name we have come against this vast army. O LORD, you are our God; do not let man prevail against you."
> **Psalm 30:2** O LORD my God, I called to you for help and you healed me.
> **Psalm 33:20** We wait in hope for the LORD; he is our help and our shield.
> **Psalm 46:1** God is our refuge and strength, an ever-present help in trouble.

Psalm 54:4 Surely God is my help; the Lord is the one who sustains me.

Psalm 121:1-2 I lift up my eyes to the hills — where does my help come from? My help comes from the LORD, the Maker of heaven and earth.

So do not fear,_____, for I am with you; do not be dismayed, _____, for I am your God, I will strengthen you, _____, and help you; I will uphold you with my righteous right hand. Isaiah 41:3

In the same way, the Spirit helps us in our weakness. We do not know what we ought to pray for, but the Spirit himself intercedes for us with groans that words cannot express. And he who searches our hearts knows the mind of the Spirit, because the Spirit intercedes for the saints in accordance with God's will. Romans 8:26-27

God is Holy

Holy: spiritually perfect or pure; sinless; deserving awe, reverence, adoration

It is very difficult to imagine or comprehend holiness. To be perfect, pure, and sinless is something no human can attain. When I focus on the fact that God's holy presence surrounds me – that I indeed am standing on holy ground – I am filled with awe. As I focus on him, I catch a glimpse of his glory, his greatness and his holiness. My spirit is lifted and filled with peace. I am humbled that such a holy God knows me and loves me. I worship and praise his holy name.

Exodus 15:11 Who among the gods is like you, O LORD? Who is like you — majestic in holiness, awesome in glory, working wonders?

Exodus 15:13 In your unfailing love you will lead the people you have redeemed. In your strength you will guide them to your holy dwelling.

1 Samuel 2:2 There is no one holy like the LORD; there is no one besides you; there is no Rock like our God.

Isaiah 5:16 But the LORD Almighty will be exalted by his justice, and the holy God will show himself holy by his righteousness.

Isaiah 6:3 And they were calling to one another: "Holy, holy, holy is the LORD Almighty; the whole earth is full of his glory."

Psalm 77:13 Your ways, O God, are holy. What god is so great as our God?

Psalm 20:6 Now I know that the LORD saves his anointed; he answers him from his holy heaven with the saving power of his right hand.

Psalms 111:9 He provided redemption for his people; he ordained his covenant forever — holy and awesome is his name.

Therefore, I urge you, _____, in view of God's mercy, to offer your body as a living sacrifice, holy and pleasing to God - this is your spiritual act of worship. Do not conform any longer to the pattern of this world, _____, but be transformed by the renewing of your mind. Then you, _____, will be able to test and approve what God's will is - his good, pleasing and perfect will. Romans 12:1-2

Exalt the Lord our God and worship at his holy mountain, for the Lord our God is holy. Psalm 99:9

God gives Hope

Hope: to desire something with confident expectation of its fulfillment

Hope is a force that keeps us moving forward. Without hope, purpose fades and the future grows dim. In God's word I find encouragement, help, wisdom, truth and so much more that fills me with hope. Even when I cannot see or understand how my situation will be resolved, I am hopeful, knowing that God has a plan and that he is working in all things to benefit those who love him. When I keep my focus on him, I can press on with confidence and with hope.

> **Psalm 62:5-6** Find rest, O my soul, in God alone; my hope comes from him. He alone is my rock and my salvation; he is my fortress, I will not be shaken.
>
> **Psalm 71:5-6** For you have been my hope, O Sovereign LORD, my confidence since my youth. From birth I have relied on you; you brought me forth from my mother's womb. I will ever praise you.
>
> **Isaiah 49:23c** ...those who hope in me (God) will not be disappointed.
>
> **Jeremiah 29:11** "For I know the plans I have for you," declares the LORD, "plans to prosper you

and not to harm you, plans to give you hope and a future."

Lamentations 3:25 The LORD is good to those whose hope is in him, to the one who seeks him.

Romans 12:12 Be joyful in hope, patient in affliction, faithful in prayer.

Romans 15:4 For everything that was written in the past was written to teach us, so that through endurance and the encouragement of the Scriptures we might have hope.

2 Thessalonians 2:16-17 May our Lord Jesus Christ himself and God our Father, who loved us and by his grace gave us eternal encouragement and good hope, encourage your hearts and strengthen you in every good deed and word.

May the God of hope fill you, _____, with all joy and peace as you, _____, trust in him, so that you, _____, may overflow with hope by the power of the Holy Spirit. Romans 15:13

We wait in hope for the Lord; he is our help and our shield. In him our hearts rejoice, for we trust in his holy name. May your unfailing love rest upon us, O Lord, even as we put our hope in you. Psalm 33:20-22

God does not Hurry
He teaches us to Wait

Hurry: to move about with haste (the act of hurrying carelessly or recklessly); to cause to occur or be done more rapidly or too rapidly; to move faster than is comfortable or natural

Wait: to stay in a place or remain in readiness or in anticipation until something expected happens

Are you in God's waiting room? Are there prayers you have prayed for days, months, even years that you have not seen answered? The scriptures are clear, that when we wait on God, he will be faithful to act and he wants good things for us. Our timetable may not be the same as his, but we can trust him that he will not act in haste. His answers are perfectly timed. It is in the waiting room that we can see our faith grow as we wait in expectation of his answer. It is there that we can tell him, "I trust you." As you pray and wait for God, find hope in him, knowing that he will not act hastily or too quickly, but in perfect timing to give you the blessing that you need.

Psalm 5:2-3 Listen to my cry for help, my King and my God, for to you I pray. In the morning, O

LORD, you hear my voice; in the morning I lay my requests before you and wait in expectation.

Psalm 27:13-14 I am still confident of this: I will see the goodness of the LORD in the land of the living. Wait for the LORD; be strong and take heart and wait for the LORD.

Psalm 37:7 Be still before the LORD and wait patiently for him; do not fret when men succeed in their ways, when they carry out their wicked schemes.

Psalm 37:34 Wait for the LORD and keep his way. He will exalt you to inherit the land; when the wicked are cut off, you will see it.

Psalm 38:15 I wait for you, O LORD; you will answer, O Lord my God.

Psalm 130:5 I wait for the LORD, my soul waits, and in his word I put my hope.

Isaiah 30:18 Yet the LORD longs to be gracious to you; he rises to show you compassion. For the LORD is a God of justice. Blessed are all who wait for him!

Isaiah 40:31 Yet those who wait for the LORD will gain new strength; they will mount up with wings like eagles, they will run and not get tired, they will walk and not become weary. (New American Standard Bible)

We wait in hope for the LORD; he is _____'s help and _____'s shield. In him our hearts rejoice, for we trust in his holy name. Psalm 33:20-21

For when you did awesome things that we did not expect, you came down, and the mountains trembled before you. Since ancient times no one has heard, no ear has perceived, no eye has seen any God besides you, who acts on behalf of those who wait for him. Isaiah 64:3-4

God does the Impossible

Impossible: incapable of being done, attained, fulfilled or occurring

As I read the scriptures about Jesus Christ, I read that he was born of a virgin, that he healed those blind from birth, fed the five thousand with a small boy's lunch, and raised the dead. He was crucified, yet was resurrected from the dead. He can change the heart of the most hardened sinner, and forgive sin, remembering it no more. All these things are such seeming impossibilities. But God does the impossible! According to the scriptures, we only must believe and be obedient to follow him. Nothing is too difficult for God. For what impossibility are you trusting him? May your focus be on the one who does the impossible.

Luke 1:26-38 In the sixth month, God sent the angel Gabriel to Nazareth, a town in Galilee, to a virgin pledged to be married to a man named Joseph, a descendant of David. The virgin's name was Mary. The angel went to her and said, "Greetings, you who are highly favored! The Lord is with you."

Mary was greatly troubled at his words and wondered what kind of greeting this might be. But the angel said to her, "Do not be afraid, Mary, you have found favor with God. You will be with child and give birth to a son, and you are to give him the name Jesus. He will be great and will be called the Son of the Most High. The Lord God will give him the throne of his father David, and he will reign over the house of Jacob forever; his kingdom will never end." "How will this be," Mary asked the angel, "since I am a virgin?" The angel answered, "The Holy Spirit will come upon you, and the power of the Most High will overshadow you. So the holy one to be born will be called the Son of God. Even Elizabeth your relative is going to have a child in her old age, and she who was said to be barren is in her sixth month. For nothing is impossible with God." "I am the Lord's servant," Mary answered. "May it be to me as you have said." Then the angel left her.

John 9:1-6 As he went along, he saw a man blind from birth. His disciples asked him, "Rabbi, who sinned, this man or his parents, that he was born blind?" "Neither this man nor his parents sinned," said Jesus, "but this happened so that the work of God might be displayed in his life. As long as it is day, we must do the work of him who sent me. Night is coming, when no one can work. While I am in the world, I am the light of the world." Having said this, he spit on the ground, made some mud with the saliva, and put it on the man's eyes. "Go," he told him, "wash in the Pool of Siloam" (this word means Sent). So the man went and washed, and came home seeing.

John 11:38-44 Jesus, once more deeply moved, came to the tomb. It was a cave with a stone laid across the entrance. "Take away the stone," he said. "But, Lord," said Martha, the sister of the dead man, "by this time there is a bad odor, for he has been there four days." Then Jesus said, "Did I not tell you that if you believed, you would see the glory of God?" So they took away the stone. Then Jesus looked up and said, "Father, I thank you that you have heard me. I knew that you always hear me, but I said this for the benefit of the people standing here, that they may believe that you sent me." When he had said this, Jesus called in a loud voice, "Lazarus, come out!" The dead man came out, his hands and feet wrapped with strips of linen, and a cloth around his face. Jesus said to them, "Take off the grave clothes and let him go."

Matthew 19:23-26 Then Jesus said to his disciples, "I tell you the truth, it is hard for a rich man to enter the kingdom of heaven. Again I tell you, it is easier for a camel to go through the eye of a needle than for a rich man to enter the kingdom of God." When the disciples heard this, they were greatly astonished and asked, "Who then can be saved?" Jesus looked at them and said, "With man this is impossible, but with God all things are possible."

Acts 2:23-24 This man was handed over to you by God's set purpose and foreknowledge; and you, with the help of wicked men, put him to death by nailing him to the cross. But God raised him from the dead, freeing him from the agony of death, because it was impossible for death to keep its hold on him.

Praise be to the God and Father of our Lord Jesus Christ! In his great mercy he has given _____ new birth into a living hope through the resurrection of Jesus Christ from the dead, and into an inheritance that can never perish, spoil or fade — kept in heaven for _____. 1 Peter 1:3-4

And without faith it is impossible to please God, because anyone who comes to him must believe that he exists and that he rewards those who earnestly seek him. Hebrews 11:6

God is our Joy

Joy: emotion evoked by well-being, success or good fortune, gladness or delight

It is easy to be joyful when things are going well, but in the scriptures, we find that we are to be joyful even when we face difficulties. How is that possible? If our sense of well-being is based on our circumstances, it is not always easy to be joyful, but if our joy is found in that which is beyond our circumstances, we can transcend our difficulties and find joy by focusing on the salvation of God. The joy that this brings gives us strength, hope, peace and gratitude. It is a joy that inspires and fulfills. It is a joy that remains, regardless of our circumstances. It is our delight as we see God at work, growing and maturing our relationship with him.

Strength - **Nehemiah 8:10** Nehemiah said, "Go and enjoy choice food and sweet drinks, and send some to those who have nothing prepared. This day is sacred to our Lord. Do not grieve, for the joy of the LORD is your strength."

His Presence - **Psalm 16:11** You have made known to me the path of life; you will fill me with joy in your presence, with eternal pleasures at your right hand.

Salvation - **Psalm 51:12** Restore to me the joy of your salvation and grant me a willing spirit, to sustain me.

His Word - **Psalm 119:111** Your statutes are my heritage forever; they are the joy of my heart.

God Alone - **Habakkuk 3:17-18** Though the fig tree does not bud and there are no grapes on the vines, though the olive crop fails and the fields produce no food, though there are no sheep in the pen and no cattle in the stalls, yet I will rejoice in the LORD, I will be joyful in God my Savior.

Jesus - **Luke 2:10** But the angel said to them, "Do not be afraid. I bring you good news of great joy that will be for all the people."

Complete - **John 15:11** I have told you this so that my joy may be in you and that your joy may be complete.

Consider it pure joy, _____, whenever you face trials of many kinds, because you know that the testing of your faith develops perseverance. Perseverance must finish its work so that you, _____, may be mature and complete, not lacking anything. James 1:2-4

You turned my wailing into dancing; you removed my sackcloth and clothed me with joy, that my heart may sing to you and not be silent. O Lord my God, I will give you thanks forever. Psalm 30:11-12

God is Kind

Kind: sympathetic; friendly; gentle; tenderhearted; generous

When we read about the life of Jesus, it is evident that his actions are a reflection of God's kindness. His acts of kindness included healing the sick, comforting those who were discouraged, spending time with children, feeding the hungry and speaking words of encouragement. It is amazing how powerful a simple act of kindness can be. A kind word of encouragement or forgiveness can be life changing. As you focus on the kindness of God, let his example inspire you to become a reflection of him.

2 Samuel 22:50-51 Therefore I will praise you, O LORD, among the nations; I will sing praises to your name. He gives his king great victories; he shows unfailing kindness to his anointed, to David and his descendants forever.

Isaiah 54:8 "In a surge of anger I hid my face from you for a moment, but with everlasting kindness I will have compassion on you," says the LORD your Redeemer.

Jeremiah 9:24 "But let him who boasts boast about this: that he understands and knows me, that

I am the LORD, who exercises kindness, justice and righteousness on earth, for in these I delight," declares the LORD.

Luke 4:40 When the sun was setting, the people brought to Jesus all who had various kinds of sickness, and laying his hands on each one, he healed them.

Luke 18:15-16 People were also bringing babies to Jesus to have him touch them. When the disciples saw this, they rebuked them. But Jesus called the children to him and said, "Let the little children come to me, and do not hinder them, for the kingdom of God belongs to such as these."

Ephesians 2:6-8 And God raised us up with Christ and seated us with him in the heavenly realms in Christ Jesus, in order that in the coming ages he might show the incomparable riches of his grace, expressed in his kindness to us in Christ Jesus. For it is by grace you have been saved, through faith — and this not from yourselves, it is the gift of God.

_____, get rid of all bitterness, rage and anger, brawling and slander, along with every form of malice. Be kind and compassionate to one another, forgiving each other, just as in Christ God forgave you, _____.
Ephesians 4:31-32

I will tell of the kindnesses of the LORD, the deeds for which he is to be praised, according to all the LORD has done for us — yes, the many good things he has done for the house of Israel, according to his compassion and many kindnesses. Isaiah 63:7

God Leads

Lead: to guide by direction or example; to go first

Imagine the chaos if the world had no leaders. Yet there are leaders of all kinds, both good and bad, with varying styles of leadership. The scriptures show that God is a loving, compassionate, leader who protects and cares for those he leads. He does not leave us during difficult times, but guides us in ways that lead us to peace. Yet he does not only lead in difficult times, he is here to lead us at all times. He goes before us – he goes first. What a comfort to know that we will not walk down an unknown path, for God walks before us. He goes first.

> **Exodus 15:13** In your unfailing love you will lead the people you have redeemed. In your strength you will guide them to your holy dwelling.
> **Psalm 77:19** Your path led through the sea, your way through the mighty waters, though your footprints were not seen.
> **Nehemiah 9:12** By day you led them with a pillar of cloud, and by night with a pillar of fire to give them light on the way they were to take.
> **Psalm 136:16** To him who led his people through the desert, his love endures forever.

Hosea 11:4 I led them with cords of human kindness, with ties of love; I lifted the yoke from their neck and bent down to feed them.

Isaiah 42:16 I will lead the blind by ways they have not known, along unfamiliar paths I will guide them; I will turn the darkness into light before them and make the rough places smooth. These are the things I will do; I will not forsake them.

Psalm 119:105 Your word is a lamp to my feet and a light for my path.

Psalm 23:2 He makes me lie down in green pastures, he leads me beside quiet waters.

Isaiah 40:11 He tends his flock like a shepherd: he gathers the lambs in his arms and carries them close to his heart; he gently leads those that have young.

Psalm 61:2 From the ends of the earth I call to you, I call as my heart grows faint; lead me to the rock that is higher than I.

Since you are _____'s rock and _____'s fortress, for the sake of your name, lead and guide _____. Psalm 31:3

But thanks be to God, who always leads us in triumphal procession in Christ and through us spreads everywhere the fragrance of the knowledge of him.
2 Corinthians 2:14

God Lifts

Lift: to raise from a lower to a higher position; to elevate; to exert effort to overcome resistance of weight

The concept of lifting fills my mind with many pictures, but one of the most vivid is of the times when I saw my husband lift our children up to sit on his shoulders when they were little. As they sat there, they felt safe and special. They were higher than all others and all their weight was on his shoulders. As a child of God, I see myself - and you - on his shoulders. I cannot get there until he lifts me up, but it is there that I can put all of my weight on him and trust him to carry me safely above all the turmoil below.

> **1 Samuel 2:8** He raises the poor from the dust and lifts the needy from the ash heap; he seats them with princes and has them inherit a throne of honor. For the foundations of the earth are the LORD's; upon them he has set the world.
>
> **Psalm 145:14** The LORD upholds all those who fall and lifts up all who are bowed down.
>
> **Job 5:11** The lowly he sets on high, and those who mourn are lifted to safety.

Psalm 30:1 I will exalt you, O LORD, for you lifted me out of the depths and did not let my enemies gloat over me.

Hosea 11:4 I led them with cords of human kindness, with ties of love; I lifted the yoke from their neck and bent down to feed them.

He lifted _____ out of the slimy pit, out of the mud and mire; He set _____'s feet on a rock and gave _____ __ a firm place to stand. Psalm 40:2

He said, "Surely they are my people, sons who will not be false to me"; and so he became their Savior. In all their distress he too was distressed, and the angel of his presence saved them. In his love and mercy he redeemed them; he lifted them up and carried them all the days of old. **Isaiah 63:8-10**

God is Light

Light: daytime, brightness, illumination, exposure to truth

It is easy to imagine a totally dark room. Most of us have experienced that at one time or another. It is very difficult, however to imagine a place with <u>no</u> darkness. It seems that there is always a shadow or a corner where it is darker. We read in **1 John 1: 5,** "This is the message we have heard from him and declare to you: God is light; in him there is no darkness at all." I realized that when I am <u>in God</u> there is <u>no</u> darkness at all. If I find myself in darkness, I have moved away from God and if I experience darkness it is time to move back close to him. I must choose to walk in his marvelous light. It is there that I will find peace and grace for everything I face.

> **Genesis 1:3** And God said, "Let there be light." and there was light. (God - creator of light)
> **Psalm 4:6b,7a,8** Let the light of your face shine upon us, O Lord. You have filled my heart with greater joy... I will lie down and sleep in peace, for you alone, O Lord, make me dwell in safety. (In God's light we have peace, joy and safety.)
> **Psalm 18:28-29** You, O Lord, keep my lamp burning; my God turns my darkness into light. With

your help I can advance against a troop; with my God I can scale a wall. (God provides all that we need. He is our light and our help.)

Psalm 27:1 The Lord is my light and my salvation - whom shall I fear? The Lord is the stronghold of my life - of whom shall I be afraid? (God's light protects us.)

Psalm 36:9 For with you is the fountain of life; in your light we see light. (When we are in him we are in his light.)

Psalm 119:105,130 Your word is a lamp to my feet and a light for my path. The unfolding of your words gives light; it gives understanding to the simple. (God's light is given through his word.)

Psalm 139:11-12 If I say, "Surely the darkness will hide me and the light become night around me," even the darkness will not be dark to you; the night will shine like the day, for darkness is as light to you. (God is light - in him there is no darkness.)

John 8:12 When Jesus spoke again to the people, he said, "I am the light of the world. Whoever follows me will never walk in darkness, but will have the light of life." (God's light came to earth - it is Jesus.)

2 Corinthians 4:6 For God, who said, "Let light shine out of darkness," made his light shine in our hearts to give us the light of the knowledge of the glory of God in the face of Christ. (When Jesus is in our heart, God's light is shining in our life and we know him.)

Revelation 21:22-23 I did not see a temple in the city, because the Lord God Almighty and the Lamb are its temple. The city does not need the sun or the moon to shine on it, for the glory of God gives it light, and the Lamb is its lamp. (The light of God will illuminate all things in Heaven.)

Righteousness and justice are the foundation of your throne; love and faithfulness go before you. Blessed is _____ who is learning to acclaim you and to walk in the light of your presence, O Lord. May _____ rejoice in your name all day long and exult in your righteousness, for you are _____'s glory and strength... Psalm 89:14-17a

But you are a chosen people, a royal priesthood, a holy nation, a people belonging to God, that you may declare the praises of him who called you out of darkness into his wonderful light. 1 Peter 2:9

God Listens

Listen: to hear something with thoughtful attention

So often we "hear" things but we are not really "listening." I praise God that not only does he hear our prayer, he listens to us as we pray. Then in his perfect wisdom, he acts in our behalf and for our good. When you pray, consider the attributes of God and take time to praise him and focus on who he is. Be still and allow God to bring to your mind those sins that hinder your fellowship with him, then confess your sin. Think about all the ways he has blessed you, from the little everyday things to the ways he has responded to your prayers. Then, with confidence in him, voice your concerns knowing that he is listening - with thoughtful attention!

Genesis 30:22 Then God remembered Rachel; he listened to her and opened her womb.

2 Kings 13:4 Then Jehoahaz sought the LORD's favor, and the LORD listened to him, for he saw how severely the king of Aram was oppressing Israel.

2 Chronicles 33:13 And when he prayed to him, the LORD was moved by his entreaty and listened to his plea; so he brought him back to Jerusalem and to his kingdom. Then Manasseh knew that the LORD is God.

Psalm 10:17 You hear, O LORD, the desire of the afflicted; you encourage them, and you listen to their cry.

Psalm 22:24 For he has not despised or disdained the suffering of the afflicted one; he has not hidden his face from him but has listened to his cry for help.

Jonah 2:2 In my distress I called to the LORD, and he answered me. From the depths of the grave I called for help, and you listened to my cry.

"For I know the plans I have for you", _____, *declares the LORD, "plans to prosper you and not to harm you,* _____, *plans to give you hope and a future. Then you will call upon me and come and pray to me, and I will listen to you,* _____. *You will seek me and find me when you seek me with all your heart." Jeremiah 29:11-13*

I cried out to him with my mouth; his praise was on my tongue. If I had cherished sin in my heart, the Lord would not have listened; but God has surely listened and heard my voice in prayer. **Psalm 66:17-19**

God is Love

Love: strong affection, desire or devotion

God's love is unfailing, enduring, abounding from generation to generation. He lavishes his love upon us and nothing can separate us from his love. Such love is hard to comprehend. His expressions of love are unending. He loves us so much that he came to earth, lived and died so that we might know him. His love gives us hope and purpose. **1 Corinthians 13:4-8a** perfectly describes God's love. God's love is patient, it is kind. It does not envy, it does not boast, it is not proud. It is not rude, it is not self-seeking, it is not easily angered, it keeps no record of wrongs. His love does not delight in evil but rejoices with the truth. It always protects, always trusts, always hopes, always perseveres. God's love never fails.

Deuteronomy 7:9 Know therefore that the LORD your God is God; he is the faithful God, keeping his covenant of love to a thousand generations of those who love him and keep his commands.

1 Chronicles 16:34 Give thanks to the LORD, for he is good; his love endures forever.

Psalm 36:5 Your love, O LORD, reaches to the heavens, your faithfulness to the skies.

Psalm 36:7 How priceless is your unfailing love! Both high and low among men find refuge in the shadow of your wings.

Psalm 103:8 The LORD is compassionate and gracious, slow to anger, abounding in love.

1 John 4:9-10 This is how God showed his love among us: He sent his one and only Son into the world that we might live through him. This is love: not that we loved God, but that he loved us and sent his Son as an atoning sacrifice for our sins.

1 John 3:1a How great is the love the Father has lavished on us, that we should be called children of God! And that is what we are!

1 John 4:16 And so we know and rely on the love God has for us. God is love. Whoever lives in love lives in God, and God in him.

Romans 8:39 Neither height nor depth, nor anything else in all creation, will be able to separate us from the love of God that is in Christ Jesus our Lord.

Let the morning bring _____ word of your unfailing love, (may) _____ put (his/her) trust in you. Show _____ __ the way (he/she) should go, for to you I lift up _____'s soul. Psalm 143:8

I pray that out of his glorious riches, he may strengthen you with power through his Spirit in your inner being, so that Christ may dwell in your hearts through faith. And I pray that you, being rooted and established in love may have power, together with all the saints, to grasp how wide and long and high and deep is the love of Christ, and to know this love that surpasses knowledge that you may be filled to the measure of all the fullness of God. Ephesians 3:16-19

God is Merciful

Merciful: forgiving; compassionate

The tender mercy of God is shown in **Luke 1:76-79** as Zechariah sang to God upon the birth of his son, John. "And you, my child, will be called a prophet of the Most High; for you will go on before the Lord to prepare the way for him, to give his people the knowledge of salvation through the forgiveness of their sins, because of the tender mercy of our God, by which the rising sun will come to us from heaven to shine on those living in darkness and in the shadow of death, to guide our feet into the path of peace." The words of his song perfectly proclaim the incredible mercy of God because of his compassion and love for us.

> **Deuteronomy 4:31** For the LORD your God is a merciful God; he will not abandon or destroy you or forget the covenant with your forefathers, which he confirmed to them by oath.
> **Psalm 6:9** The LORD has heard my cry for mercy; the LORD accepts my prayer.
> **Isaiah 55:7** Let the wicked forsake his way and the evil man his thoughts. Let him turn to the LORD, and he will have mercy on him, and to our God, for he will freely pardon.

Jeremiah 3:12 Go, proclaim this message toward the north: " 'Return, faithless Israel,' declares the LORD, 'I will frown on you no longer, for I am merciful,' declares the LORD, 'I will not be angry forever.'"

Daniel 9:18 Give ear, O God, and hear; open your eyes and see the desolation of the city that bears your Name. We do not make requests of you because we are righteous, but because of your great mercy.

Micah 7:18 Who is a God like you, who pardons sin and forgives the transgression of the remnant of his inheritance? You do not stay angry forever but delight to show mercy.

Matthew 5:7 Blessed are the merciful, for they will be shown mercy.

Luke 1:50 His mercy extends to those who fear him, from generation to generation.

Ephesians 2:4-5 But because of his great love for us, God, who is rich in mercy, made us alive with Christ even when we were dead in transgressions — it is by grace you have been saved.

For you, _____, do not have a high priest who is unable to sympathize with your weaknesses, but you have one who has been tempted in every way, just as you are, yet was without sin. Therefore, _____, approach the throne of grace with confidence, so that you may receive mercy and find grace to help you in your time of need. Hebrews 4:15-16

Praise be to the God and Father of our Lord Jesus Christ! In his great mercy he has given us new birth into a living hope through the resurrection of Jesus Christ from the dead, and into an inheritance that can never perish, spoil or fade

— kept in heaven for you, who through faith are shielded by God's power until the coming of the salvation that is ready to be revealed in the last time. 1 Peter 1:3-5

God is Near

Near: close by

There are times when I experience the presence of God and I know that he is near. At other times I feel alone and he seems far away. Yet in those times when he seems far away, I realize that he has not moved away, it is I who have moved away from him. Still, God is God at all times regardless of our position. God longs for us to be near to him, for he is always near. He is ready to help, to comfort, to redeem. Rejoice! You are not alone. God is near.

Deuteronomy 4:7 What other nation is so great as to have their gods near them the way the LORD our God is near us whenever we pray to him?

Psalm 75:1 We give thanks to you, O God, we give thanks, for your Name is near; men tell of your wonderful deeds.

Psalm 145:18 The LORD is near to all who call on him, to all who call on him in truth.

Isaiah 50:8 He who vindicates me is near. Who then will bring charges against me? Let us face each other! Who is my accuser? Let him confront me!

Isaiah 55:6 Seek the LORD while he may be found; call on him while he is near.

Jeremiah 23:23 "Am I only a God nearby," declares the LORD, "and not a God far away?"

Lamentations 3:56-58 You heard my plea: "Do not close your ears to my cry for relief." You came near when I called you, and you said, "Do not fear." O Lord, you took up my case; you redeemed my life.

Rejoice in the Lord always, _____. I will say it again: Rejoice! Let your gentleness, _____, be evident to all. The Lord is near, _____. Do not be anxious about anything, _____, but in everything, by prayer and petition, with thanksgiving, present your requests to God. Philippians 4:4-6

But as for me, it is good to be near God. I have made the Sovereign LORD my refuge; I will tell of all your deeds. Psalm 73:28

God makes things New

New: different from that which has been before

Although there are times when we take something old and try to fix it, spruce it up, or make it better, we cannot take something old and make it new. Yet, that is what God does in so many ways. He alone is able to give us a new spirit, a new attitude, and a new life. He replaces the old with the new. What an encouragement to know that God is able to create a change that not only improves, but makes things new.

> **Isaiah 43:18,19** Forget the former things; do not dwell on the past. See, I am doing a new thing! Now it springs up; do you not perceive it? I am making a way in the desert and streams in the wasteland.
>
> **Psalm 40:3** He put a new song in my mouth, a hymn of praise to our God. Many will see and fear and put their trust in the LORD
>
> **Isaiah 65:17** Behold, I will create new heavens and a new earth. The former things will not be remembered, nor will they come to mind.
>
> **Lamentations 3:22-23** Because of the LORD's great love we are not consumed, for his compassions

never fail. They are new every morning; great is your faithfulness.

Romans 6:4 We were therefore buried with him through baptism into death in order that, just as Christ was raised from the dead through the glory of the Father, we too may live a new life.

2 Corinthians 5:17 Therefore, if anyone is in Christ, he is a new creation; the old has gone, the new has come!

1 Peter 1:3 Praise be to the God and Father of our Lord Jesus Christ! In his great mercy he has given us new birth into a living hope through the resurrection of Jesus Christ from the dead.

I will sprinkle clean water on you, _____, and you will be clean; I will cleanse you, _____, from all your impurities and from all your idols. I will give you a new heart and put a new spirit in you, _____; I will remove from you your heart of stone and give you a heart of flesh. And I will put my Spirit in you, _____, and move you to follow my decrees and be careful to keep my laws. Ezekiel 36:25-27

Then I saw a new heaven and a new earth, for the first heaven and the first earth had passed away, and there was no longer any sea. I saw the Holy City, the New Jerusalem, coming down out of heaven from God, prepared as a bride beautifully dressed for her husband. And I heard a loud voice from the throne saying, "Now the dwelling of God is with men, and he will live with them. They will be his people, and God himself will be with them and be their God. He will wipe every tear from their eyes. There will be no more death or mourning or crying or pain, for the old order

of things has passed away." He who was seated on the throne said, "I am making everything new!" Then he said, "Write this down, for these words are trustworthy and true." Revelation 21:1-6

God is Patient

Patient: bearing pains or trials calmly or without complaint; forbearance under provocation or strain

How many times, when you are faced with difficulty have you cried out for patience? We long for patience in order to find peace and calm, yet it is in those very trials that we learn how to be patient. Patience is given the opportunity to emerge when we are tested. Because it is a fruit of the Spirit, it is an attribute of God and as we develop this attribute we will be more like God. God is patient. I am glad he is.

2 Peter 3:9 The Lord is not slow in keeping his promise, as some understand slowness. He is patient with you, not wanting anyone to perish, but everyone to come to repentance.

Hebrews 12:1-3 Therefore, since we are surrounded by such a great cloud of witnesses, let us throw off everything that hinders and the sin that so easily entangles, and let us run with perseverance the race marked out for us. Let us fix our eyes on Jesus, the author and perfecter of our faith, who for the joy set before him endured the cross, scorning its shame, and sat down at the right hand of the throne of God. Consider him who endured such opposition from sinful men, so that you will not grow weary and lose heart.

Galatians 5:22 But the fruit of the Spirit is love, joy, peace, patience, kindness, goodness, faithfulness...

1 Corinthians 13:4 Love is patient, love is kind. It does not envy, it does not boast, it is not proud.

Psalm 37:34a Wait for the LORD and keep his way. He will exalt you to inherit the land; when the wicked are cut off, you will see it.

Be patient, then, _____, until the Lord's coming. See how the farmer waits for the land to yield its valuable crop and how patient he is for the autumn and spring rains. You too, _____, be patient and stand firm, because the Lord's coming is near. James 5:7-8

Therefore, as God's chosen people, holy and dearly loved, clothe yourselves with compassion, kindness, humility, gentleness and patience. Bear with each other and forgive whatever grievances you may have against one another. Forgive as the Lord forgave you. And over all these virtues put on love, which binds them all together in perfect unity. Colossians 3:12-14

God is our Peace

Peace: state of calm; freedom from strife or discord; harmony in personal relationship

God desires that we experience peace. Peace of heart, peace of mind, peace of spirit. Though we experience many difficulties and storms in life, the peace of God transcends them all. Truly, we can have peace in the middle of the storm when we remain fully focused on God. God is our peace.

> **Psalm 29:11** The LORD gives strength to his people; the LORD blesses his people with peace.
> **Psalm 119:165** Great peace have they who love your law, and nothing can make them stumble.
> **Proverbs 16:7** When a man's ways are pleasing to the LORD, he makes even his enemies live at peace with him.
> **Isaiah 26:3** You will keep in perfect peace him whose mind is steadfast, because he trusts in you.
> **Isaiah 32:17** The fruit of righteousness will be peace; the effect of righteousness will be quietness and confidence forever.
> **1 Corinthians 14:33a** For God is not a God of disorder but of peace.

Philippians 4:7 And the peace of God, which transcends all understanding, will guard your hearts and your minds in Christ Jesus.

Isaiah 54:10 Though the mountains be shaken and the hills be removed, yet my unfailing love for you will not be shaken nor my covenant of peace be removed, says the Lord, who has compassion on you.

Peace I leave with you, _____; my peace I give you. I do not give to you as the world gives. Do not let your heart be troubled, _____, and do not be afraid. John 14:27

May the God of peace, who through the blood of the eternal covenant brought back from the dead our Lord Jesus, that great Shepherd of the sheep, equip you with everything good for doing his will, and may he work in us what is pleasing to him, through Jesus Christ, to whom be glory for ever and ever. Amen. Hebrews 13:20-21

God Protects

Protect: to cover or shield from exposure, injury or destruction; to guard

Flowing out from God's love is his protection. The beautiful passage found in Psalm 91 is very special to me. This is the passage that my father read over and over as he experienced combat in World War II. When I hear the stories of how he landed on the beach on D-Day 3, drove over icy fields filled with mines, and slowly crossed Europe for two years facing the enemy, I am amazed at God's protection that preserved his life. Had he not returned, I would never have been born. God's love protects. We must run to him and dwell in his shelter. It is there that we are safe.

> **Proverbs 18:10** The name of the LORD is a strong tower; the righteous run to it and are safe.
> **Proverbs 2:7-8** He holds victory in store for the upright, he is a shield to those whose walk is blameless, for he guards the course of the just and protects the way of his faithful ones.
> **2 Thessalonians 3:3** But the Lord is faithful, and he will strengthen and protect you from the evil one.
> **Psalm 91** He who dwells in the shelter of the Most High will rest in the shadow of the Almighty.

I will say of the LORD, "He is my refuge and my fortress, my God, in whom I trust." Surely he will save you from the fowler's snare and from the deadly pestilence. He will cover you with his feathers, and under his wings you will find refuge; his faithfulness will be your shield and rampart. You will not fear the terror of night, nor the arrow that flies by day, nor the pestilence that stalks in the darkness, nor the plague that destroys at midday. A thousand may fall at your side, ten thousand at your right hand, but it will not come near you. You will only observe with your eyes and see the punishment of the wicked. If you make the Most High your dwelling — even the LORD, who is my refuge —then no harm will befall you, no disaster will come near your tent. For he will command his angels concerning you to guard you in all your ways; they will lift you up in their hands, so that you will not strike your foot against a stone. You will tread upon the lion and the cobra; you will trample the great lion and the serpent. "Because he loves me," says the LORD, "I will rescue him; I will protect him, for he acknowledges my name. He will call upon me, and I will answer him; I will be with him in trouble, I will deliver him and honor him. With long life will I satisfy him and show him my salvation."

Do not withhold your mercy from _____, O LORD; may your love and your truth always protect _____.
Psalm 40:11

Love is patient, love is kind. It does not envy, it does not boast, it is not proud. It is not rude, it is not self-seeking, it is not easily angered, it keeps no record of wrongs. Love does not delight in evil

but rejoices with the truth. It always protects, always trusts, always hopes, always perseveres. Love never fails. 1 Corinthians 13:4-8a

God Quiets

Quiet: free of turmoil and agitation; untroubled; characterized by tranquility; to make secure by freeing from all questions or challenges

There are times when the noise of life becomes overwhelming. Our soul and spirit long for quiet and rest from turmoil. God is the one who can calm the turmoil and restore the quiet we seek. He commands the turmoil as seen in the scripture when he calms the seas and casts out demons. His paths lead to peace and quiet. He quiets us with his love. In the midst of turmoil he asks us to be still, focus on him, and experience the quite that he alone can give.

> **Psalm 76:7-9** You alone are to be feared. Who can stand before you when you are angry? From heaven you pronounced judgment, and the land feared and was quiet— when you, O God, rose up to judge, to save all the afflicted of the land.
> **Psalm 23:2-3a** He makes me lie down in green pastures, he leads me beside quiet waters, He restores my soul.
> **Mark 4:39** He got up, rebuked the wind and said to the waves, "Quiet! Be still!" Then the wind died down and it was completely calm.

Luke 4:35 Be quiet!" Jesus said sternly. "Come out of him!" Then the demon threw the man down before them all and came out without injuring him.

Isaiah 32:17 The fruit of righteousness will be peace; the effect of righteousness will be quietness and confidence forever.

The LORD your God is with you, _____, he is mighty to save. He will take great delight in you, _____, he will quiet you _____, with his love, he will rejoice over you, _____, with singing. Zephaniah 3:17

This is what the Sovereign LORD, the Holy One of Israel, says: "In repentance and rest is your salvation, in quietness and trust is your strength." Isaiah 30:15a

Be still, and know that I am God; I will be exalted among the nations, I will be exalted in the earth. Psalm 46:10

God Rescues

Rescue: to free or save from danger, imprisonment or evil

There are times when we are trapped, physically, mentally, emotionally or spiritually, and we desperately need to be rescued. As you go through difficult moments, days, or times, remember to look to God to rescue you. He is the one who is able and he waits to hear your cries to him for help. As he did for the Israelites, he wants to rescue from captivity (of thoughts, of difficulties, of Satan's powers) and free you to a place of peace and plenty.

> **Exodus 3:7-9** The LORD said, "I have indeed seen the misery of my people in Egypt. I have heard them crying out because of their slave drivers, and I am concerned about their suffering. So I have come down to rescue them from the hand of the Egyptians and to bring them up out of that land into a good and spacious land, a land flowing with milk and honey — the home of the Canaanites, Hittites, Amorites, Perizzites, Hivites and Jebusites. And now the cry of the Israelites has reached me, and I have seen the way the Egyptians are oppressing them."
>
> **Numbers 10:9** When you go into battle in your own land against an enemy who is oppressing you,

sound a blast on the trumpets. Then you will be remembered by the LORD your God and rescued from your enemies.

1 Samuel 22:17-19 He reached down from on high and took hold of me; he drew me out of deep waters. He rescued me from my powerful enemy, from my foes, who were too strong for me. They confronted me in the day of my disaster, but the LORD was my support.

Daniel 6:26-28 "I issue a decree that in every part of my kingdom people must fear and reverence the God of Daniel. For he is the living God and he endures forever; his kingdom will not be destroyed, his dominion will never end. He rescues and he saves; he performs signs and wonders in the heavens and on the earth. He has rescued Daniel from the power of the lions." So Daniel prospered during the reign of Darius and the reign of Cyrus the Persian.

Colossians 1:12-14 ... giving thanks to the Father, who has qualified you to share in the inheritance of the saints in the kingdom of light. For he has rescued us from the dominion of darkness and brought us into the kingdom of the Son he loves, in whom we have redemption, the forgiveness of sins.

2 Timothy 4:17-19 But the Lord stood at my side and gave me strength, so that through me the message might be fully proclaimed and all the Gentiles might hear it. And I was delivered from the lion's mouth. The Lord will rescue me from every evil attack and will bring me safely to his heavenly kingdom. To him be glory for ever and ever. Amen.

Isaiah 46:4 Even to your old age and gray hairs I am he; I am he who will sustain you. I have made you and I will carry you; I will sustain you and I will rescue you.

"Because _____ loves me," says the LORD, "I will rescue _____; I will protect _____, for _____ acknowledges my name. _____ will call upon me, and I will answer_____; I will be with _____ in trouble, I will deliver_____ and honor _____." Psalm 91:14-15

Grace and peace to you from God our Father and the Lord Jesus Christ, who gave himself for our sins to rescue us from the present evil age, according to the will of our God and Father, to whom be glory for ever and ever. Amen. Galatians 1:3-5

God is the Solution
From worry to peace

Solution: an answer or process of solving a problem

Worry: to feel or experience concern or anxiety; choke, strangle; struggle, torment; implies incessant goading or attack that drives one to desperation

Peace: a state of tranquility or quiet, security or calm

There are times when we face difficulties and finding a solution seems impossible. It is sort of like trying to solve a difficult math problem. Many times, when we first see the problem, we have no idea how to find the solution. First we are filled with doubt that may lead to fear or even anger and soon we are so tied up in all these emotions that we see no way to solve the problem. It is the same with the problems we face everyday, yet the solution lies in focusing on God and seeking the peace that only he can give. Read the scriptures that flow from a place of worry to peace. As you face uncertainties and difficulties remain fully focused on God. He is the solution.

Matthew 6:25, 27 Therefore I tell you, do not worry about your life, what you will eat or drink;

or about your body, what you will wear. Is not life more important than food, and the body more important than clothes? Who of you by worrying can add a single hour to his life?

1 Peter 5: 7 Cast all your anxiety on him because he cares for you.

Psalm 4:8 I will lie down and sleep in peace, for you alone, O LORD, make me dwell in safety.

Psalm 29:11 The LORD gives strength to his people; the LORD blesses his people with peace.

Psalm 119:165 Great peace have they who love your law, and nothing can make them stumble.

Isaiah 26:3 You will keep in perfect peace him whose mind is steadfast, because he trusts in you.

John 14:27 Peace I leave with you; my peace I give you. I do not give to you as the world gives. Do not let your hearts be troubled and do not be afraid.

Philippians 4:7 And the peace of God, which transcends all understanding, will guard your hearts and your minds in Christ Jesus.

Cast your cares on the Lord, _____, and he will sustain you, _____; he will never let the righteous fall. Psalm 55:22

The Lord turn His face toward you and give you peace. Numbers 6:26

God is Strong

Strong: showing great power; having the capacity for endurance; having many resources; able to resist and endure attack

When a child is fearful, often they run to their father, knowing that they will be safe in their father's arms because he is strong. When we pray, it gives us peace and assurance if we focus on the strength of God. He is strong. We are safe when we are in his presence. He is always near. He is able to rescue us and protect us. Rather than focusing on your weakness, focus on his strength.

> **Deuteronomy 3:24** O Sovereign Lord, you have begun to show to your servant your greatness and your strong hand. For what god is there in heaven or on earth who can do the deeds and mighty works you do?
>
> **Proverbs 18:10** The name of the Lord is a strong tower; the righteous run to it and are safe.
>
> **I Corinthians 1:25** For the foolishness of God is wiser than man's wisdom, and the weakness of God is stronger than man's strength.
>
> **Psalm 89:8 and 13** O Lord God Almighty, who is like you? You are mighty, O Lord, and your faithful-

ness surrounds you. Your arm is endued with power; your hand is strong, your right hand exalted.

Psalm 89:15-17 Blessed are those who have learned to acclaim you, who walk in the light of your presence, O Lord. They rejoice in your name all day long; they exult in your righteousness. For you are their glory and strength, and by your favor you exalt our horn.

Be strong and courageous, _____. Do not be afraid or terrified...for the Lord your God goes with you, _____; He will never leave you, _____, nor forsake you. *Deuteronomy 31:6*

But he said to me, "My grace is sufficient for you, for my power is made perfect in weakness." Therefore I will boast all the more gladly about my weaknesses, so that Christ's power may rest on me. That is why, for Christ's sake, I delight in weaknesses, in insults, in hardships, in persecutions, in difficulties. For when I am weak, then I am strong. 2 Corinthians 12:9-10

God is Trustworthy

Trustworthy: dependable; reliable; worthy of placing confidence in, or to put confidently in charge

Putting our full trust in God requires a knowledge of who he is. When we learn of his attributes, it becomes clear that he is trustworthy. His love is unfailing, and his mercies never cease. He replaces our weakness with his strength and his plans are perfect. He will never leave us or forsake us and he is King of Kings and Lord of Lords. He is worthy of our trust. Come boldly before him and rest in his care.

Psalm 9:10 Those who know your name will trust in you, for you, LORD, have never forsaken those who seek you.

Psalm 19:7 The law of the LORD is perfect, reviving the soul. The statutes of the LORD are trust-worthy, making wise the simple.

Psalm 22:4-5 In you our fathers put their trust; they trusted and you delivered them. They cried to you and were saved; in you they trusted and were not disappointed.

Isaiah 25:8-9 He will swallow up death forever. The Sovereign LORD will wipe away the tears from all faces; he will remove the disgrace of his people

from all the earth. The LORD has spoken. In that day they will say, "Surely this is our God; we trusted in him, and he saved us. This is the LORD, we trusted in him; let us rejoice and be glad in his salvation."
Isaiah 28:16 So this is what the Sovereign LORD says: "See, I lay a stone in Zion, a tested stone, a precious cornerstone for a sure foundation; the one who trusts will never be dismayed."

Carefully read the following passage of scripture and pause to focus on God who is trustworthy.

Psalm 23 The LORD is my shepherd; I shall not be in want. He makes me lie down in green pastures, he leads me beside quiet waters, he restores my soul. He guides me in paths of righteousness for his name's sake. Even though I walk through the valley of the shadow of death, I will fear no evil, for you are with me; your rod and your staff, they comfort me. You prepare a table before me in the presence of my enemies. You anoint my head with oil; my cup overflows. Surely goodness and love will follow me all the days of my life, and I will dwell in the house of the LORD forever.

Trust in the Lord with all your heart, _____, and lean not on your own understanding; in all your ways acknowledge him, _____, and he will make your paths straight. Proverbs 3:5-6

Find rest, O my soul, in God alone; my hope comes from him. Trust in him at all times, O people; pour out your hearts to him, for God is our refuge. Psalm 62:5,8

God is Unfailing

Unfailing: constant; unflagging (tireless); everlasting; inexhaustible; infallible, sure

Every day we see things around us that are failing. We hear of the failing economy. We see in the news those who fail to obey the laws of the land and the laws of God. We hear of or experience failing health. But when we focus on God, we see our source of unfailing strength, hope, and help. The scriptures witness to his unfailing promises and emphasize his unfailing righteousness and unfailing love for us. When we focus our heart on God, we experience the depth of his unfailing nature.

Joshua 23:14 Now I am about to go the way of all the earth. You know with all your heart and soul that not one of all the good promises the LORD your God gave you has failed. Every promise has been fulfilled; not one has failed.

1 Kings 8:56 Praise be to the LORD, who has given rest to his people Israel just as he promised. Not one word has failed of all the good promises he gave through his servant Moses.

1 Chronicles 28:20 David also said to Solomon his son, "Be strong and courageous, and do the work.

Do not be afraid or discouraged, for the LORD God, my God, is with you. He will not fail you or forsake you until all the work for the service of the temple of the LORD is finished."

Psalm 89:27-29 I will also appoint him my first-born, the most exalted of the kings of the earth. I will maintain my love to him forever, and my covenant with him will never fail. I will establish his line forever, his throne as long as the heavens endure.

Isaiah 51:6 Lift up your eyes to the heavens, look at the earth beneath; the heavens will vanish like smoke, the earth will wear out like a garment and its inhabitants die like flies. But my salvation will last forever, my righteousness will never fail.

Lamentations 3:22 Because of the LORD's great love we are not consumed, for his compassions never fail.

Zephaniah 3:5 The LORD within her is righteous; he does no wrong. Morning by morning he dispenses his justice, and every new day he does not fail; yet the unrighteous know no shame.

Isaiah 54:10 "Though the mountains be shaken and the hills be removed, yet my unfailing love for you will not be shaken nor my covenant of peace be removed," says the LORD, who has compassion on you.

*The LORD will guide_____ always; He will satisfy _
_____'s needs in a sun-scorched land and will strengthen
_____'s frame. _____ will be like a well-watered
garden, like a spring whose waters never fail. Isaiah 58:11*

May your unfailing love rest upon us, O LORD, even as we put our hope in you. Psalm 33:22

God is Victorious

Victorious: the state of having triumphed; one who overcomes in a battle or struggle

What could be a more difficult battle than overcoming sin and overcoming death? We all experience these struggles in our lives, yet we are promised to be victorious in each of those battles. The evidence of our victory is the risen Savior, Jesus Christ. We have no power to defeat the enemy, yet through his Son, God gives us the victory and through him, we are victorious. Claim the victory each moment - each day - and praise him, for God is victorious!

> **Deuteronomy 20:4** For the LORD your God is the one who goes with you to fight for you against your enemies to give you victory.
>
> **2 Samuel 22:36-37** You give me your shield of victory; you stoop down to make me great. You broaden the path beneath me, so that my ankles do not turn.
>
> **Psalm 60:12** With God we will gain the victory, and he will trample down our enemies.
>
> **Proverbs 2:6-8** For the LORD gives wisdom, and from his mouth come knowledge and understanding. He holds victory in store for the upright,

He is a shield to those whose walk is blameless, for he guards the course of the just and protects the way of his faithful ones.

Proverbs 21:30-31 There is no wisdom, no insight, no plan that can succeed against the LORD. The horse is made ready for the day of battle, but victory rests with the LORD.

1 Corinthians 15:54-57 When the perishable has been clothed with the imperishable, and the mortal with immortality, then the saying that is written will come true: "Death has been swallowed up in victory." "Where, O death, is your victory? Where, O death, is your sting?" The sting of death is sin, and the power of sin is the law. But thanks be to God! He gives us the victory through our Lord Jesus Christ.

May the LORD answer you, _____, when you are in distress; may the name of the God of Jacob protect you. May he give you, _____, the desire of your heart and make all your plans succeed. We will shout for joy when you, _____, are victorious and will lift up our banners in the name of our God. Psalm 20:1,4-5a

I do not trust in my bow, my sword does not bring me victory; but you give us victory over our enemies, you put our adversaries to shame. In God we make our boast all day long, and we will praise your name forever. Psalm 44:6-8

God is Willing

Willing: acting, giving, consenting readily, gladly and voluntarily

Each day we are faced with choices that we must make. Sometimes we are faced with difficulties that are overwhelming. Just as Jesus did in the garden, we must make a choice to willingly follow God, though at times it leads to a personal cross we must bear. The question we must answer is, "Are you willing to follow the Christ of the Cross?"

This may seem quite heavy, but remember what followed. Jesus now sits at the right hand of the Father and reigns as King of Kings and Lord of Lords. May it give you hope to know that the cross precedes the crown. God so desired for us to experience the crown, that he willingly went to the cross. I pray that you will focus on how much God loves you and his willingness to have fellowship with you at great cost.

John 1:1,14 In the beginning was the Word, and the Word was with God, and the Word was God. He was with God in the beginning. The Word became flesh and made his dwelling among us. We have seen his glory, the glory of the One and Only, who came from the Father, full of grace and truth.

Matthew 8:1-3 When he came down from the mountainside, large crowds followed him. A man with leprosy came and knelt before him and said, "Lord, if you are willing, you can make me clean." Jesus reached out his hand and touched the man. "I am willing," he said. "Be clean!" Immediately he was cured of his leprosy.

Luke 22:41-43 He withdrew about a stone's throw beyond them, knelt down and prayed, "Father, if you are willing, take this cup from me; yet not my will, but yours be done." An angel from heaven appeared to him and strengthened him.

Luke 23:33-34 When they came to the place called the Skull, there they crucified him, along with the criminals — one on his right, the other on his left. Jesus said, "Father, forgive them, for they do not know what they are doing." And they divided up his clothes by casting lots.

John 3:16 For God so loved the world that he (willingly) gave his one and only Son, that whoever believes in him shall not perish but have eternal life.

Do not cast _____ from your presence or take your Holy Spirit from _____. Restore to_____ the joy of your salvation and grant _____ a willing spirit, to sustain _____. Psalm 51:11-12

...and live a life of love, just as Christ loved us and (willingly) gave himself up for us as a fragrant offering and sacrifice to God. Ephesians 5:2

God is Wise

Wise: having or showing good judgment; the ability to deal with persons or situations rightly, based on a broad range of experience and understanding; to see; to know

U nlike the rulers of this world who have limited wisdom, the God of the universe has perfect wisdom. What a tragedy it would be if God, who is sovereign, were not wise. Our lives would be quite different if the one who manages the universe did not have good judgment, the ability to deal with situations rightly, could not see from the beginning to the end of his plan, or could not show unconditional love, compassion and forgiveness. We are blessed to be children of the one true wise God. Because he is wise, we can put our hope, faith and trust in him in every situation.

> **2 Chronicles 9:23** All the kings of the earth sought audience with Solomon to hear the wisdom God had put in his heart.
> **Job 12:13** To God belong wisdom and power; counsel and understanding are his.
> **Proverbs 3:19** By wisdom the LORD laid the earth's foundations, by understanding he set the heavens in place.

Psalm 104:24 How many are your works, O LORD! In wisdom you made them all; the earth is full of your creatures.

Proverbs 2:6 For the LORD gives wisdom, and from his mouth come knowledge and understanding.

1 Corinthians 1:25 For the foolishness of God is wiser than man's wisdom, and the weakness of God is stronger than man's strength.

Romans 11:33 Oh, the depth of the riches of the wisdom and knowledge of God! How unsearchable his judgments, and his paths beyond tracing out!

Romans 16:27 To the only wise God be glory forever through Jesus Christ! Amen.

I have not stopped giving thanks for you, _____, remembering you in my prayers. I keep asking that the God of our Lord Jesus Christ, the glorious Father, may give you, _____, the Spirit[j] of wisdom and revelation, so that you may know him better. I pray also that the eyes of your heart may be enlightened in order that you, _____, may know the hope to which he has called you, (and) the riches of his glorious inheritance in the saints. Ephesians 1:16-18

Praise be to the name of God for ever and ever; wisdom and power are his. He changes times and seasons; he sets up kings and deposes them. He gives wisdom to the wise and knowledge to the discerning. He reveals deep and hidden things; he knows what lies in darkness, and light dwells with him. Daniel 2:20-22

Fully In Focus

The following is a summary of the attributes of God illustrated in this book. I pray that your faith will be strong and you will be encouraged as you focus on him.

God alone is *able* to do more than I could ever think or imagine. God *abounds* in love and faithfulness. God *binds our wounds* and heals the brokenhearted. God is *boundless* having no limits. God *breathes* into us both spiritual and physical life. God *cares* for us.

God *comforts* us in all our troubles. God rises to show us *compassion.* God *defends* us from the oppressor. God gives us eternal *encouragement* and good hope. God's love, faithfulness and righteousness *endures* through all generations. God *equips* us with everything for doing his will. The *exact* representation of God's glory is Jesus Christ.

God is *faithful* to all his promises. God says, *"Fear not!"* God *fills* us with joy and eternal pleasures. When God is our *focus* we experience perfect peace. God *forgives* our sin. God knows us perfectly for he *formed the mold.* God gives *freedom* to those in captivity. God *gives* all that we need. The earth is filled with God's *glory.* God is *good.* God *guides* us in his truth. God *heals* us completely. Surely God is our *help.* The Lord our God is *holy.* Those who *hope* in God will not be disappointed. God does not *hurry* or act in haste. Nothing is *impossible* with God. The *joy* of God is our strength. God shows everlasting, unfailing *kindness.* God *leads* us in triumphal procession. God *lifts* up all who are bowed down. God is *light.* In him there is no darkness. God *listens* to our cry. God is *love.* God is *merciful* and his mercies never cease. God is *near* to all who call on him. God makes all things *new.* God is *patient* not wanting anyone to perish. God is the source of *peace* that passes all understanding. God *protects* the way of his faithful ones from the evil one. God *quiets* us with his love. God will sustain and *rescue* us even into old age. God is the *solution* to subtracting worry and multiplying peace. When we are weak, God is *strong.* God is *trustworthy* and those who trust in him will never be dismayed. God's love and faithfulness are *unfailing.* When God fights the battle, he is *victorious.* God was *willing* to come to earth and become flesh and go to the cross to die for our sin. God is the source of *wisdom,* knowledge and understanding.

May God be praised for his perfect love for us as shown by his attributes and may we keep him *fully in focus.*

LaVergne, TN USA
30 October 2010
202800LV00002B/2/P